New Directions for
Higher Education

Betsy O. Barefoot
Jillian L. Kinzie
Co-editors

How Ideal Worker Norms Shape Work-Life for Different Constituent Groups in Higher Education

Lisa Wolf-Wendel
Kelly Ward
Amanda M. Kulp
Editors

Number 176 • Winter 2016
Jossey-Bass
San Francisco

How Ideal Worker Norms Shape Work-Life for Different Constituent Groups in Higher Education
Lisa Wolf-Wendel, Kelly Ward, Amanda M. Kulp
New Directions for Higher Education, no. 176
Co-editors: Betsy O. Barefoot and Jillian L. Kinzie

NEW DIRECTIONS FOR HIGHER EDUCATION, (Print ISSN: 0271-0560; Online ISSN: 1536-0741), is published quarterly by Wiley Subscription Services, Inc., a Wiley Company, 111 River St., Hoboken, NJ 07030-5774 USA.
Postmaster: Send all address changes to NEW DIRECTIONS FOR HIGHER EDUCATION, John Wiley & Sons Inc., C/O The Sheridan Press PO Box 465, Hanover, PA 17331 USA.

Information for subscribers
New Directions for Higher Education is published in 4 issues per year. Institutional subscription prices for 2017 are:
Print & Online: US$454 (US), US$507 (Canada & Mexico), US$554 (Rest of World), €363 (Europe), £285 (UK). Prices are exclusive of tax. Asia-Pacific GST, Canadian GST/HST and European VAT will be applied at the appropriate rates. For more information on current tax rates, please go to www.wileyonlinelibrary.com/tax-vat. The price includes online access to the current and all online back files to January 1st 2013, where available. For other pricing options, including access information and terms and conditions, please visit www.wileyonlinelibrary.com/access.

Delivery Terms and Legal Title
Where the subscription price includes print issues and delivery is to the recipient's address, delivery terms are **Delivered at Place (DAP)**; the recipient is responsible for paying any import duty or taxes. Title to all issues transfers FOB our shipping point, freight prepaid. We will endeavour to fulfil claims for missing or damaged copies within six months of publication, within our reasonable discretion and subject to availability.

Back issues: Single issues from current and recent volumes are available at the current single issue price from cs-journals@wiley.com.

Disclaimer
The Publisher and Editors cannot be held responsible for errors or any consequences arising from the use of information contained in this journal; the views and opinions expressed do not necessarily reflect those of the Publisher and Editors, neither does the publication of advertisements constitute any endorsement by the Publisher and Editors of the products advertised.

Publisher: New Directions for Student Leadership is published by Wiley Periodicals, Inc., 350 Main St., Malden, MA 02148-5020.

Journal Customer Services: For ordering information, claims and any enquiry concerning your journal subscription please go to www.wileycustomerhelp.com/ask or contact your nearest office.
Americas: Email: cs-journals@wiley.com; Tel: +1 781 388 8598 or +1 800 835 6770 (toll free in the USA & Canada).
Europe, Middle East and Africa: Email: cs-journals@wiley.com; Tel: +44 (0) 1865 778315.
Asia Pacific: Email: cs-journals@wiley.com; Tel: +65 6511 8000.
Japan: For Japanese speaking support, Email: cs-japan@wiley.com.
Visit our Online Customer Help available in 7 languages at www.wileycustomerhelp.com/ask

Production Editor: Poornita Jugran (email: pjugran@wiley.com).

Wiley's Corporate Citizenship initiative seeks to address the environmental, social, economic, and ethical challenges faced in our business and which are important to our diverse stakeholder groups. Since launching the initiative, we have focused on sharing our content with those in need, enhancing community philanthropy, reducing our carbon impact, creating global guidelines and best practices for paper use, establishing a vendor code of ethics, and engaging our colleagues and other stakeholders in our efforts. Follow our progress at www.wiley.com/go/citizenship

View this journal online at wileyonlinelibrary.com/journal/he

Wiley is a founding member of the UN-backed HINARI, AGORA, and OARE initiatives. They are now collectively known as Research4Life, making online scientific content available free or at nominal cost to researchers in developing countries. Please visit Wiley's Content Access - Corporate Citizenship site: http://www.wiley.com/WileyCDA/Section/id-390082.html

Printed in the USA by The Sheridan Group.

Address for Editorial Correspondence: Co-editors, Betsy Barefoot and Jillian L. Kinzie, New Directions for Higher Education, Email barefoot@jngi.org

Abstracting and Indexing Services
The Journal is indexed by Academic Search Alumni Edition (EBSCO Publishing); Higher Education Abstracts (Claremont Graduate University); MLA International Bibliography (MLA).

Cover design: Wiley
Cover Images: © Lava 4 images | Shutterstock

For submission instructions, subscription and all other information visit: wileyonlinelibrary.com/journal/he

Contents

Editors' Notes

Work and family concerns are increasingly on the radar of colleges and universities. These concerns emerge out of workplace norms suggesting that for employees and students to be successful, they must be "ideal workers" dedicated solely to their careers. As a part of this singular focus on work, ideal workers are expected to limit attention to nonwork pursuits including children or at least have a spouse to meet family needs (Acker, 1990; Bailyn, Drago, & Kochan, 2001). The workplace remains organized around traditional male, White, and middle-class life patterns of decades past in which women tended to home responsibilities and men worked outside the home (Williams, 2000). With the prevalence of dual-career couples today, ideal worker models disadvantage both men and women since such workplace expectations clearly can be at odds with the demands of family life.

Researchers suggest that work-life policies are a way to remedy the structural inequities and to improve the work experience for faculty and students (Finkel & Olswang, 1996; Goulden, Frasch, & Mason, 2009; Quinn, 2011; Sallee, 2012). The academy has slowly adopted work-life policies, but these policies have had mixed success, in part, because workplace norms and subcultures pressure individuals to conform to the ideal worker model, leaving people fearful of relying on policy (Grant, Kennelly, & Ward, 2000; Thompson, 2008; Ward & Wolf-Wendel, 2012).

Ideal worker-norm pressures can be especially challenging given the number of women in the workplace today and the number of men and women who juggle responsibilities as members of dual-career couples. In 2008, 79% of married or partnered employees were members of dual-career couples (Galinsky, Aumann, & Bond, 2008). In more than 70% of two-parent households with children, both parents now work outside the home (Harrington, Van Deusen, & Ladge, 2010). Without the support of a full-time homemaker, ideal worker norms, such as working full time and taking little time off, become difficult to meet (Moen, 2005). Ideal worker norms are frequently unspoken, and individuals are left to figure out how to navigate ambiguous demands. For a variety of reasons, the inability to meet unspoken norms can lead women and men who want to play a role in caregiving to opt out of careers, fail to advance, or compromise personal goals such as having children at a biologically appropriate time (Armenti, 2004).

NEW DIRECTIONS FOR HIGHER EDUCATION, no. 176, Winter 2016 © 2016 Wiley Periodicals, Inc.
Published online in Wiley Online Library (wileyonlinelibrary.com) • DOI: 10.1002/he.20205

Although most of the existing research has focused on the ways in which faculty experience ideal worker pressure in the academy (e.g., Sallee, 2012; Thompson, 2008; Ward & Wolf-Wendel, 2012), this volume broadens the scope of the existing conversation to consider how a variety of actors in the academy, including faculty, staff, and undergraduate and graduate students, understand, interpret, strategize, work with, and resist the ideal worker model. These varying perspectives are important because the ideal worker is often context dependent, and people may navigate ideal worker norms differently within the same institution or department given their relationship to the context. As the number of tenure-track positions in the academy declines and calls for greater accountability across higher-education rise, each of these constituent groups may find itself feeling compelled to conform to ideal worker norms. Addressing workplace norms calls for shifts and changes in the attitudes and beliefs of employees at all levels across the academy. Research that only focuses on one group of employees fails to address these macroscopic perspectives.

The intent of this volume is to explore perceptions of the ideal worker in higher education and the ways in which various campus constituents experience and interpret ideal worker expectations. The ideal worker model provides a useful frame for thinking about the norms that operate to shape the behavior of constituents in differing contexts. We examine how visions of the ideal worker vary for faculty, administrators, and students. We also discuss the ways in which the model, with its context-dependent norms, can constrain employees' ability to balance personal and professional lives. Finally, the chapters will promote dialogue, analysis, and critique of academic workplace cultures as a way to promote further action and policy. Most importantly, the chapters offer recommendations for how institutions and policymakers might modify ideal worker norms in the academy.

The volume primarily addresses two overarching questions:

1. How do ideal worker norms shape work and family life for members of the campus community?
2. How do individuals in positions across the academy understand, conform to, and resist ideal worker norms in light of family responsibilities?

As higher education continues to evolve, answers to these questions have important implications for the work-life balance experiences of employees, the diversification of a quality academic workplace, and the future of the academy. The goal of the volume is to engage in critical dialogue regarding ideal worker norms present in the academy as well as to provide recommendations for institutions regarding how to make work expectations transparent and attainable for diverse individuals with a range of work-life commitments.

Chapter Outline

The first chapter in this volume explores how mid-career tenured women faculty members, who are mothers and academics, manage multiple roles. The chapter is based on a longitudinal, qualitative study. The perspectives offered contribute to how ideal worker norms shape family formation and family life throughout the academic career for tenured academic mothers. The researchers use life-course perspectives and feminist theory to challenge ideal worker norms and institutional contexts that support such norms. We start with this chapter because so much of the research on work-life focuses on women faculty members on the tenure track; this chapter adds a new perspective by focusing on women in mid-career stages.

The second chapter, drawing on an analysis of existing literature, examines how work norms and work-life concerns affect the growing number of non-tenure-track faculty. The chapter demonstrates the importance of understanding the diversity of contingent faculty experiences and of underemployment to explain their work lives rather than notions of the ideal worker.

Chapter 3 focuses on the work-life experiences of male and female administrators at a private, doctoral institution where ideal worker norms constrained administrator behavior. Administrators with and without some degree of informal workplace flexibility desired to challenge ideal worker norms in their areas and replace existing norms with a work environment that emphasized results, not time spent at work.

Chapter 4 looks at the consequences of ideal worker norms for graduate student-parents in both higher education and student affairs master's degree programs. Using Schein's (2004) levels of culture, the chapter considers the ways that programmatic structures and interactions with faculty and peers reflect and reproduce a culture across graduate programs that privileges the norm of the always-working and engaged student, thereby creating barriers to full participation for students with children.

Chapter 5 considers how undergraduate single mothers navigate ideal student expectations. Undergraduates are an important population to consider because they represent the first step in the academic pipeline. Their experiences have the potential to influence who enters graduate school and who becomes administrators or professors in higher education. Relying on a review of current literature, the chapter looks at the ways undergraduates who are single mothers are counter to the "ideal student" norms. Policy and best-practice recommendations, based upon the literature, conclude the chapter.

Based on a quantitative national study of doctoral degree recipients, Chapter 6 focuses on the presence of career-related resources that doctoral students attain during graduate school, and the influence of those resources on PhD-earning mothers' attainment of tenure-track faculty jobs at U.S. higher-education institutions.

The final chapter integrates the themes throughout the chapters to explore what ideal worker norms mean for future research, policy, and practice. Building upon the conclusions of each chapter, the author offers important policy recommendations that are related to the groups discussed and that provide a path forward for colleges and universities wanting to attract and retain a diverse student body and workforce.

Lisa Wolf-Wendel
Kelly Ward
Amanda Kulp
Editors

References

Acker, J. (1990). Hierarchies, jobs, bodies: A theory of gendered organizations. *Gender and Society, 4*(2), 139–158.

Armenti, C. (2004). May babies and posttenure babies: Maternal decisions of women professors. *The Review of Higher Education, 27*(2), 177–231.

Bailyn, L., Drago, R., & Kochan, T. (2001). *Integrating work and family life: A holistic approach.* Cambridge, MA: Massachusetts Institute of Technology, Sloan School of Management.

Finkel, S. K., & Olswang, S. G. (1996). Child rearing as a career impediment to women assistant professors. *The Review of Higher Education, 19*(2), 123–139.

Galinsky, E., Aumann, K., & Bond, J. T. (2008). *Times are changing: Gender and generation at work and at home.* New York, NY: Families and Work Institute. Retrieved from http://www.familiesandwork.org/site/research/reports/Times_Are_Changing.pdf

Goulden, M., Frasch, K., & Mason, M. (2009). *Staying competitive: Patching America's leaky pipeline in the sciences.* Berkeley: University of California, Berkeley Center on Health, Economic, & Family Security and The Center for American Progress, i–49.

Grant, L., Kennelly, I., & Ward, K. B. (2000). Revisiting the gender, marriage, and parenthood puzzle in scientific careers. *Women's Studies Quarterly, 28*(1–2), 62–85.

Harrington, B., Van Deusen, F., & Ladge, J. (2010). *The new dad: Exploring fatherhood within a career context.* Newton, MA: Boston College Center for Work & Family.

Moen, P. (2005). Beyond the career mystique: "Time in," "time out," and "second acts." *Sociological Forum, 20,* 187–208.

Quinn, K. (2011). Graduate and professional students' opinion on work-family balance in academic faculty careers. *Journal of the Professoriate, 5*(1), 99–120.

Schein, E. (2004). *Organizational culture and leadership* (3rd ed.). San Francisco, CA: Jossey-Bass.

Sallee, M. W. (2012). The ideal worker or the ideal father: Organizational structures and culture in the gendered university. *Research in Higher Education, 53*(7), 782–802.

Thompson, C. A. (2008). Barriers to the implementation and usage of work-life policies. In S. A. Y. Poelmans & P. Caligiuri (Eds.), *Harmonizing work, family, and personal life: From policy to practice* (pp. 19–38). Cambridge, UK: Cambridge University Press.

Ward, K., & Wolf-Wendel, L. (2012). *Academic motherhood: How faculty manage work and family.* New Brunswick, NJ: Rutgers University Press.

Williams, J. (2000). *Unbending gender: Why family and work conflict and what to do about it.* New York, NY: Oxford University Press.

NEW DIRECTIONS FOR HIGHER EDUCATION • DOI: 10.1002/he

LISA WOLF-WENDEL *is a professor of higher education and associate dean for Research and Graduate Studies, School of Education, University of Kansas.*

KELLY WARD *is professor of higher education and department chair of Educational Leadership and Counseling Psychology in the College of Education at Washington State University.*

AMANDA KULP *is a program manager in the office of institutional research and planning at the University of Kansas.*

NEW DIRECTIONS FOR HIGHER EDUCATION • DOI: 10.1002/he

This chapter explores how mid-career tenured women faculty, who are mothers and academics, manage multiple roles. The women represent faculty at a variety of institutional types and in a variety of disciplines. The chapter looks at these experiences in light of ideal worker norms.

Academic Motherhood: Mid-Career Perspectives and the Ideal Worker Norm

Kelly Ward, Lisa Wolf-Wendel

Topics related to academic motherhood have generated a spate of research (cf., Mason, Wolfinger, & Goulden, 2013; Sallee, 2014; Ward & Wolf-Wendel, 2012). The primary focus of existing research is related to faculty members with young children and early-career faculty, and, in general, mid-career faculty are overlooked as a focus of study (Baldwin, DeZure, Shaw, & Moretto, 2008). In contrast, the focus of this chapter is work, family, and mid-career faculty. The chapter examines how careers and family life intersect throughout the careers of academic women. Accordingly we ask: How do work and family concerns evolve throughout the career? What impact does family life have on career decisions? How do career decisions shape family life?

Related Literature

Colleges and universities concerned with the recruitment and retention of a high-quality and diverse faculty have created "family-friendly" policies (Lester & Sallee, 2009). Faculty members themselves have also brought forth work and family topics for institutional consideration. Concomitant to institutional and individual attention, there has also been an increase in research related to work and family. Topics include pipeline perspectives (e.g., Mason et al., 2013), academic fathers (Sallee, 2014), and policy environments (Lester & Sallee, 2009). There are books and essays dedicated to highlighting personal experiences of academic life from the perspective of mothers (e.g., Evans & Grant, 2008), fathers (e.g., Marotte, Reynolds, & Savarese, 2011), and mothers in different disciplines (e.g., Monosson, 2008). There are also volumes that look beyond traditional notions of

New Directions for Higher Education, no. 176, Winter 2016 © 2016 Wiley Periodicals, Inc.
Published online in Wiley Online Library (wileyonlinelibrary.com) • DOI: 10.1002/he.20206

parenting and professing by calling attention to experiences related to single parenting, postpartum depression, and same-sex couples (e.g., O'Brien Hallstein & O'Reilly, 2013).

A few "truths" are evident from looking at the research related to work, family, and the academic career: (a) tenure-track academic careers are "greedy" and call for total commitment to faculty life, and ideal workers are rewarded (Hochschild, 1989); (b) parenting, and more directly mothering, is demanding, and being a "good" mother calls for an intensive, and preferably exclusive, commitment to the mother role (O'Brien Hallstein & O'Reilly, 2013); (c) women have greater access to the academic workplace than they have had historically, but access has not converted to advancement and equity; and, (d) many colleges and universities have created and updated work–family policies (e.g., parental leave and tenure-clock stop policies), yet these policies tend to be underutilized for fear of bias (Ward & Wolf-Wendel, 2012) and have not had desired outcomes (Antecol, Bedard, & Stearns, 2016).

Many researchers, including ourselves and others throughout this volume, use the construct of the "ideal worker" to frame work and family topics. Ideal workers are dedicated to the job, meaning they are not supposed to take into consideration things that are non-job related (i.e., family). Historically, ideal workers have been men. Women (and White women in particular), have made headway in bucking norms that historically kept them at home, and men have made considerable progress with more involvement with families and home. Yet, contemporary norms associated with motherhood and parenting still assume a dedication to family that excludes devotion to work. Academic women can find themselves in a bind that stands at the intersection of ideal worker norms that assume a complete focus on work, intensive mothering norms that assume total dedication to family, and societal norms that grant unprecedented access to women in the workplace while limiting what they can achieve if they want to be a professional and a parent. Ideal worker norms expect women to approach work as though they do not have children, and intensive mothering norms expect women to parent as if they do not have careers (Roshell, 2016). O'Brien Hallstein and O'Reilly (2013) refer to this conflict as a "distinct-to-academia 'perfect storm' of difficult and almost-impossible-to-meet challenges" where academic mothers try to have and manage it all (p. 3). It is this "perfect storm" that makes issues associated with the advancement and equity of academic women so complex to address. The challenges women face at work are compounded by expectations at home as well as by society. In spite of progress, gender stereotypes and norms in home and work spheres stymy the progress of women as professors.

What is missing from existing research is attention to how work and family evolve throughout the academic career and contribute to the underrepresentation of senior level women. Although there is research on midcareer faculty (e.g., Baldwin et al., 2008), the focus is on general career

issues, not work-life topics. Current research and campus demographic re-
alties suggest that women do not progress in their careers as faculty or in
their progression to leadership positions at the same rate as their male colleagues (Ceci, Ginther, Kahn, & Williams, 2014; Mason et al., 2013). In
part, the lag is attributed to work and family conflicts, yet there has been
little empirical investigation of work, family, and mid-career stages of academic life.

Theoretical Perspectives

The research that provides the data for this chapter is guided by two conceptual strands—life-course perspectives of human development and feminist
theory. We draw on life-course perspectives given the focus of the interaction of work and family and how life changes over time (Han & Moen,
1999). A life-course perspective recognizes that work and family are not
static and that a comprehensive analysis calls for looking at work *and* family throughout life stages. Women, in particular, lead "linked lives" when it
comes to work and family (Elder, 1994). A life-course approach allows for
an integrated instead of sequential analysis of work and family (Jacobs &
Winslow, 2004). A life-course perspective is particularly relevant for looking at academic careers in that most faculty once established tend to stay in
the faculty career. This perspective allows us to consider career and family
dynamics at all career stages.

A feminist perspective examines work, family, and faculty life amid
the context of gender norms that are shaped by history and power
(Donovan, 2012) as well as societal and organizational structures (Allan,
2011). Change, from a feminist perspective, requires alterations of structures rather than of individuals. These assumptions about women and gender undergird different theoretical approaches that further define feminism.
Given the diversity in viewpoints about feminism, we draw upon liberal and
poststructural views.

A liberal view of feminism posits that women should be entitled to
the same "natural rights" as men (Donovan, 2012). Such a perspective is
foundational to the concept of equal opportunity and is evident in many of
the social and organizational policies that have been the focus for women
in the workplace (Acker, 1987). Within the liberal view, women should be
able to participate fully in society and in work free from traditionally defined gender roles. Foundational to liberal feminism is the notion that men
and women are equal and that policies and practices level the playing field
for men and women to participate and compete on equal terms (Donovan,
2012). A liberal view is evident in organizations that seek to create gender-
equitable workplaces. The thinking goes that if institutions create more equitable policies and workplaces, then women will perform and progress
in ways that mirror men's progress. Liberal feminism is the predominant
view for campuses striving to improve the conditions of the workplace for

women and is the basis for creating most workplace family-friendly policy. Our research and that of others (e.g, Sallee, 2014; Antecol et al., 2016), however, shows that adding more women or creating more policies is not enough to generate equal career outcomes for men and women. A liberal view helps identify gender inequality, but it fails to dig into nuanced understandings of equity and gender.

Feminist poststructuralism as an analytical tool digs deeper and focuses on gender in relationship to societal structures, language, power, and discourse. Such a view allows for the examination of women's experiences relative to social practices and power by looking at language, power, difference, and subjectivity (Allan, 2011; Allan & Ropers-Huilman, 2009; Weedon, 1996). Feminist poststructuralism questions the status quo and seeks to address inequitable social systems and divisions of labor from the perspective of gender. A poststructuralist view helps to uncover assumptions about the workplace and how gender shapes participation. Theory is a way to look at how overlapping identities interact and shape work and personal life choices. We use liberal and poststructural feminist lenses as well as the life-course perspective to make sense of the experiences of mid-career faculty as mothers and professors.

Research Methods

The study data are based on a longitudinal study about work and family for female faculty. In the first phase of the project, we interviewed 120 early-career faculty about their experiences as new professors and new mothers. The second phase of the study is based on interviews with 88 of the original 120 faculty. The third phase is ongoing and is based on interviews with 44 of the faculty in the original sample (faculty we label as "mid mid-career"). The faculty members in the third phase of the study are from community colleges, comprehensive institutions, liberal arts colleges, and research universities. The participants are from an array of disciplines. Although the focus of this chapter is the third phase of the study, longitudinal perspectives shape overall understanding.

Interviews were tape-recorded and transcribed and then analyzed using the constant comparative approach (Strauss & Corbin, 1990). This analysis approach helped us identify "the patterns, themes, and categories of analysis that come from the data; they emerge out of the data rather than being imposed on them prior to data collection and analysis" (Patton, 1980, p. 306). Mindful of gender and gender relations evident in the poststructural and liberal views of feminism (Allan, 2011; Donovan, 2012), we looked at the themes that emerged from the analysis to see how policy, gender relations and norms (including ideal worker norms), and organizational structures shaped the work-life integration experience of the women in the study. The life-course perspective (Han & Moen, 1999) provided a lens to look at the findings from a macroscopic view of work and family and investigated how synergy and conflicts shape the experience of the women in the study.

Findings

The findings focus on three main themes—"leaning back," autonomy, and views from the middle. Following is an overview of each theme and related analysis. The findings cut across discipline and institutional context.

Leaning Back for Work and Family Balance. In Sandberg's (2013) often-cited book *Lean In*, she encourages women to "lean in" to their positions in an effort to increase the representation for women in senior level positions. A predominant finding from the study at the mid mid-career stage is that participants are opting to "lean back." In general, they are not focused on career advancement in terms of promotion (for those not already promoted to full professor) or administration. As more established faculty who are in a stage of parenting older, more independent children (mostly high school or college age), there is time to "not be so stressed at home and work." As one study participant shared, "I have a more relaxed approach about my work and my family now than I did before." Ideal worker norms are present in the workplace, but as established faculty, the women in the study are more likely to observe the norms than feel bound by them as they did early career. As a faculty member from a research university shared: "My new [junior] colleagues feel like they have to work all the time to be successful. They feel immense pressure. My job is to mentor to help people succeed. I'm not in it like I used to be."

In the second phase of the study, we noted involvement in service commitments as a pathway to leadership (Ward & Wolf-Wendel, 2012). What we found present in the third phase of the study is that women were not generally pursuing promotion and/or leadership positions. Instead, using the terminology of Sandberg (2013), they were "leaning back." There were two elements to the decision to not pursue leadership roles. The first related to having already done service or leadership, and the second related to witnessing unpleasant leadership cultures and not wanting to participate.

The study participants are an active group of faculty who have participated in service and leadership positions consistent with senior faculty roles. For some participants, there was the feeling that they had already "done their share" in terms of leadership. When asked about her desire to move into a leadership role, one participant captured the leaning-back notion perfectly: "I did my share. I was involved in several initiatives for a while and wasn't rewarded for it. It's time for someone else to step up." The findings show the idea of "turn taking" to be prevalent; when the participants' "turn" (as chair or leader of graduate studies or director of assessment) was completed, they were not interested in any additional leadership positions. In part, this was shaped by family responsibilities. As one person shared, "I would work really hard and move up, but my kids are only home for a limited time and I don't want to spend my time that way." Leadership roles are greedy in terms of time and can infringe on work and family balance. Participants observed that to be successful as a leader means "working all the time." The two faculty members in the study who are now in senior level administrative positions, felt pressure to work "all the time" and be "on call 24/7." Ideal worker norms are present in senior leadership positions or at least observed as present by student participants. As one respondent shared: "I felt that [being in leadership] really impeded my ability to get work done. Just the stress." She further described how leadership roles do not always honor family obligations. "When it's time to go. I need to go. I got to get out, got to get out right now, folks. I can't hold on one more minute, because I get fined if I'm late to pick up my kid."

We also found that managing work and family was not just about children, but also about addressing the needs of aging parents. About half of the participants were actively engaged in caring for their parents either close to home or at a distance. "My mother-in-law moved here which has been great. She's a big help with getting my son to practice and she likes to hang out with us." She went on, "we help take care of her and her house which adds to my daily routine." Another participant shared how she and her sister take turns to care for aging parents: "My parents live in California. My sister and I take turns going to see them to make sure they have what they need at their house. As they get older it's a lot of worry." Being more established in their careers allowed participants time for care work related to children and/or aging parents.

Participants also felt they had to conform to ideal worker norms for promotion to full professor, which served as a deterrent. One person likened going up for professor to going up for tenure: "I'm torn between the book contract and current home-life stability. It feels like a repeat choice to the decisions I had to make to get my first book to get tenure" She felt at a "juncture," and if she did not get a book contract, she would be giving up "future promotional opportunities. I aspire to full professor, but have not been in a rush due to having a young child at home. The process seems too exhausting right now." She lamented going back to an intensive writing process that was incongruous with having a family and was not immediately planning to go up for promotion to full professor. Since pursuing promotion to full professor is an option in the academy rather than a requirement, we found that some faculty opted out of the full-professor promotion process because they could.

Autonomous Lives.   A major finding from the earlier phases of the study suggests that autonomy was a double-edged sword for academic women—on the one hand, academic life affords high levels of autonomy where people can organize their time and manage schedules largely independently. The flip side of autonomy was expressed in the first two stages of the study in terms of "never-ending workloads" (Ward & Wolf-Wendel, 2012). There was a general sense of never doing enough in terms of teaching, research, or service. In this third phase of the study, the participants are more established and they are claiming their autonomy and shaping their work lives to focus on primary areas of interest. As one participant told us, "I've done it all [in terms of service, administration, promotion], and at this point I really want to just focus on teaching and my students." The autonomy granted by academic careers allows faculty to focus on the areas of their work they find most gratifying. The autonomy also allows faculty to abandon ideal worker norms and find a level of integration between work and family that is "not as stressed as when I was a new professor and a new mother."

Autonomy is also related to time. Generally, as established faculty, participants created their schedules. "I have a pretty good deal here. As far as being able to set my schedule and work within the time of dropping off my kids and being able to pick them up." A similar view of time and autonomy contributed to attitudes about promotion, "I don't *have* to go up for promotion, and I don't want to give up the time." This mindset was especially prevalent in environments where the reward for going up for promotion was limited. The findings make clear that faculty were working hard; what autonomy granted was how to focus their work.

Views From the Middle.   In general, the findings suggest a general lack of interest in moving into senior levels either in terms of promotion to academic rank (if they were not already promoted to full professor) or movement into leadership or administrative positions. In contrast to the first theme, the focus here is not so much on having a balance between work and family, but instead, a focus on wanting to "avoid conflict" and "stay out of politics and political messes." Promotion and leadership are viewed as processes that require a level of commitment that is not attractive (e.g., "People work all the time and that's not very interesting to me.") and a work setting that can be negative and not very welcoming ("I've worked in leadership roles and at this point I'm just saying 'no thanks.' The jobs can be thankless and I found it to be not very welcoming in terms of work environment."). There is a general perception that the amount of physical and emotional investment required for senior level administrative roles is not attractive, compelling, or "worth it" and there are benefits to being established (i.e., in the middle), but not at the most senior levels.

Research about leadership pipelines suggests that women are not likely to move into leadership at the same rate as their male colleagues based on anticipated challenges (Sandberg, 2013). One reason offered from the study findings was related to work norms. Comments like "you have to work all the time" in reference to administration were commonplace. With regard to going up for full professor, we heard different renditions of the comment— "it's messy and I don't want to do it [go up for full professor]" or "it's political and not worth it." Being in the middle and mid-career affords a lens to look at where the participants had been (i.e., on the tenure track) and a lens about where they could go.

As was highlighted in the finding about leaning back, in some instances once they were in leadership positions, women were not interested in moving forward in terms of traditional career advancement. As one participant explained, "Once was enough. I did it once and was not treated very well." Similarly with promotion, women faculty members were deterred from going up for full professor based on what other people had experienced or what they themselves experienced going up for tenure. One person thinking about promotion to full professor commented, "In my department there are 32 [faculty] and only 2 women are full professors. Many women are turned down. It's very gender biased against women. There are sexist remarks. Maybe with retirement of the old guard, things may improve."

For this woman, going up for promotion to full professor was viewed as a political process that is dictated by who she is—a woman—and, incidentally was a process to be avoided. The women in the study were sufficiently established in their careers to believe they knew the terrain and to know if they want to be part of the process of advancement. Related, we also found that people waited to go up for promotion until a significant retirement took place or until there were changes in the guidelines for promotion so the process would be more manageable. As an example we heard from one person, "After 12 years as an associate professor I finally got promoted. I couldn't go through what I went through for tenure so I had to wait for a key retirement."

A benefit of being established and in the middle (hierarchically and career wise) is exploring other positions when desired. Most campuses have no shortage of opportunities for people to pursue formal leadership (e.g., chair and associate dean) or high-level involvement service positions (e.g., faculty senate). The women in the study who were considering senior leadership positions saw expanded involvement in service and administrative positions as keys to moving into higher-level positions. For example, we heard from one participant: "The ideal thing is to become a dean in your own college and see if you like it. It is much smoother and easier to transition back [to faculty]." Another shared that her experience leading accreditation for her college created a pathway to leadership:

> My heart and soul is in the faculty, but I also believe that if faculty want good leadership, we have to be willing to move up. When I finished accreditation for my college, which I was the leader of, and I kind of knew the insides and outs of the college and how it functions, from the fiscal to the whole gamut, the two women vice presidents at the time, said, "buy yourself a suit, you are on your way."

Her experience points out the importance of mentorship to women as they plan and think about their careers. Mentors provide career advice, help pave the way, and provide a sounding board for career and life issues.

Work and family concerns for the women at the mid mid-career stage can complicate the ascent to leadership. We heard repeatedly about not wanting to uproot families for potential new opportunities. Most participants in the study stayed on the campus where they started their careers, but depending on campus context, moving up in leadership sometimes meant moving out. As one participant told us: "I basically felt forced to leave if I wanted to rise, and I struggled with that greatly." Part of the struggle had to do with uprooting her family. Even from participants with older children, we heard that moving would be disruptive either to children, parents, dual careers, or to leaving a community in which a person is established.

The overall findings of the study suggest that work and family concerns continue to exist as people move into the middle part of their career. For those in early careers, the findings centered on taking care of young children. Early mid-career attention was on navigating family needs as children get older—typically related to car pools and balancing work needs with changing family needs. In this phase of the study—the mid mid-career stage—findings tended toward reclaiming "balance" and intentionally choosing what to do and what not to do. We now turn to further discussion of the findings from a life-course and feminist perspective.

Discussion and Analysis.   The study uses two different lenses as tools of analysis—a life-course perspective and feminist theory. The findings in the study make clear that the career decisions women make are tied to where they are in family life. Women lead "linked lives" when it comes to work and family. Decisions about one domain clearly shape decisions made in the other (Elder, 1994). The findings related to career advancement, in particular, illustrate the link between work and family. For women in a leadership trajectory, life beyond work clearly influences career decisions. This was particularly evident in career decisions that would require moving. In a traditional framework, and a life dictated by ideal worker norms, work comes first. A rational cost–benefit analysis takes place and, if warranted, a career move is made. The findings here show that career decisions are complicated by family obligations including children, even when they get older, and aging parents. A life-course approach points to an integrated instead of sequential analysis of work and family (Jacobs & Winslow, 2004).

A feminist view of the findings points to the gendered nature of work and family life especially for women. Liberal perspectives of feminism suggest that the implementation of policies and structures will help level the playing field for women to progress (Donovan, 2012). If institutional structures to eliminate discrimination on the basis of gender are in place, within a liberal frame the assumption is that decisions made by individual women to participate, to get promoted, and to pursue leadership opportunities will be made in a gender-neutral context. Such a view suggests that there is equal access to unbounded choices and that given options people will make rational choices. Classic notions of agency also assume people make the best decisions for themselves, families, and careers given a certain set of options

(O'Meara & Campbell, 2011). What this perspective fails to consider is that women are not making choices independent of their families including parents, children, and spouses or independent of their gendered expectations of what a woman should do at home and at work.

Choices about promotion and administration are shaped by gendered expectations and contexts. We were surprised by the number of women in the study who opted out of the promotion process and lacked interest in administrative positions even when they were already exercising leadership. In part, these decisions were a consequence of wanting to avoid politics and ideal worker norms. Conventional wisdom asserts that as more women enter the pipeline, more women will advance into higher positions. The findings from this research suggest that pipeline progression can be thwarted by the gendered intersections of work and family.

A poststructural feminist view recognizes the need for structural changes at home and at work to remedy the underrepresentation of women in senior faculty and administrative positions. When looking at the findings, it is easy to cite personal choice as the reason women are not progressing into senior positions. Academic life, especially once a person is established, is filled with choices related to what research to pursue, service positions to take, presentations to make, and even the choice to go up for promotion (or not). It is easy to look at individual women and the choices they make as key factors inhibiting greater representation of women at senior levels. We see an alternate and more nuanced view of these choices. A feminist perspective, especially one in line with a poststructural view, highlights that the pipeline itself and the social structures that have created the pipeline need to be addressed rather than focusing on the participants in the pipeline and the choices they make.

Implications for Policy and Practice

The findings from this study suggest that on its own, career advancement is not taking place in ways that will close gender gaps. Although the interaction between work and family is part of the deterrent for advancement, there is also concern about ideal worker norms and gendered expectations. The findings suggest that for women's careers to progress, the implementation of policy and practice as well as the critical examination of how gendered norms manifest structurally and organizationally need to take place. We offer the following recommendations for consideration.

Update Campus Policies.   Promotion and tenure policies need to focus on getting tenure *and* on promotion to full professor. Full professor status is often a prerequisite for full participation in senior levels of administration. Data indicate that despite increases for women in early stages of the pipeline as assistant professors, leaks in the pipeline result in fewer women reaching full professor (National Center for Education Statistics, 2011). In addition to policies, there needs to be ongoing review of campus-based data to see who is using the policies and related career outcomes.

Leadership Development Programs.   Although not enough on their own, leadership-development programs help prepare people for leadership positions. Progressive leadership preparation and development programs for aspiring and current leaders need to include explicit discussions about gender, work and family, and ideal worker norms. Nomination processes need to be critically examined, be broad and inclusive, and rely on multiple methods of selection ranging from nomination to personal invitation to open calls.

Leaders as Role Models and Mentors.   Current leaders need to understand ideal worker norms and how these unquestioned practices are gendered and affect the leaders themselves and others. Mentors provide essential career guidance. Women often do not recognize their own leadership potential and wait to be tapped for leadership. Mentors and leaders should highlight how there is no single pathway up the career ladder nor a single model for successful leadership.

It's Not Just About Women.   It is crucial to include men and women in discussions about mentorship, gender, leadership, and work–family related topics. Too often, women are targeted for special programs that reinforce individual perspectives. It is critical to promote awareness on the part of all colleagues (men and women) about how they spend their time at work and at home. Policy and practice need to look gender and the experiences of men and women.

Conclusion

The findings from the study suggest that participants manage to navigate work and home lives to forge successful careers and satisfying lives. Their trajectories, however, may not correspond with what academic institutions hope will happen to create gender equity at senior levels. Some of the women in the study might be seen as having "stalled out" on their pathway up the academic ladder. Yet, they do not see themselves as deadwood, as unproductive, or as unsuccessful. Rather, they see themselves as making strategic choices that allow them to fulfill the range of obligations they face at home and at work.

The representation of women faculty in the highest ranks and in leadership positions is part of an ongoing conversation in higher education. The fact that this sample of women faculty is not making the progress through the ranks that one might hope for speaks as much to the experiences of these women as it does to the institutional climates and cultures in which they work. Recognizing the limitations of the pipeline metaphor (i.e., that it is linear and fixed), we nonetheless suggest that the most productive way to look at the results of this study is not by examining what is wrong with these women but rather by interrogating what structures exist in society and higher education impede their progress, including ideal worker norms that deter women from wanting to progress to senior levels. In other words, rather than looking at fixing the drops of water (the entrants into the pipeline), we ought to spend our energies fixing the pipe itself. We end this chapter with our assertion that water will leak if the pipe is broken.

References

Acker, S. (1987). Feminist theory and the study of gender and education. *International Review of Education, 33*(4), 419–435.

Allan, E. J. (2011). Women in higher education. *ASHE Higher Education Report, 37*(1). San Francisco, CA: Jossey-Bass.

Allan, E., Iverson, S. V., & Rop ers-Huilman, R. (2009). *Reconstructing policy in higher education: Feminist poststructural perspectives.* London, England: Routledge.

Antecol, H., Bedard, K., & Stearns, J. (2016). Equal but inequitable: Who benefits from gender-neutral tenure clock stopping policies?" *IZA Discussion Paper No. 9904.* Retrieved from https://docs.google.com/viewer?a=v&pid=sites&srcid= ZGVmYXVsdGRvbWFpbnxzdGVhcm5zamV8Z3g6NGI3YWExYjg2NjIwZWYyYg

Baldwin, R., Dezure, D., Shaw, A., & Moretto, K. (2008). Mapping the terrain of mid-career faculty at a research university: Implications for faculty and academic leaders. *Change, 40,* 46–55.

Ceci, S. J., Ginther, D. K., Kahn, S., & Williams, W. M. (2014). Women in academic science: explaining the gap. *Psychological Science in the Public Interest, 15*(3).

Donovan, J. (2012). *Feminist theory: The intellectual traditions.* New York, NY: Continuum.

Elder, G. H. (1994). Time, human agency and social change: Perspectives on the life course. *Social Psychology Quarterly, 57,* 4–15.

Evans, E., & Grant, C. (Eds.). (2008). *Mama, PhD: Women write about motherhood and academic life.* New Brunswick, NJ: Rutgers University Press.

Han, S.K., & Moen, P. (1999). Work and family over time: A life course approach. *The ANNALS of the American Academy of Political and Social Science, 562,* 98–110.

Hochschild, A. (1989). *The second shift: Working parents and the revolution at home.* New York, NY: Viking Press.

Jacobs, J., & Winslow, S. (2004). The academic life course, time pressures and gender inequality. *Community, Work & Family, 7,* 143–161.

Lester, J., & Sallee, M. (2009). *Establishing the family-friendly campus: Models for effective practice.* Sterling, VA: Stylus.

Marotte, M. R., Reynolds, P., & Savarese, R. J. (Eds.). (2011). *Papa, PhD: Essays on fatherhood by men in the academy.* New Brunswick, NJ: Rutgers University Press.

Mason, M, Wolfinger, N. H., & Goulden, M. (2013). *Do babies matter: Gender in the ivory tower.* New Brunswick, NJ: Rutgers University Press.

Monosson, E. (Ed.). (2008). *Motherhood, the elephant in the laboratory: Women scientists speak out.* Ithaca, NY: Cornell University Press.

National Center for Education Statistics (NCES). (2011). *Digest of educational statistics: 2011.* Washington, DC: Author.

O'Brien Hallstein, D. L., & O'Reilly, A. (2013). *Academic motherhood in a post-second wave context: Challenges, strategies, and possibilities,* Toronto, Canada: Demeter.

O'Meara, K., & Campbell, C. (2011). Faculty sense of agency in decisions about work and family. *The Review of Higher Education, 3,* 447–476.

Patton, M. Q. (1980). *Qualitative evaluation methods.* Beverly Hills, CA: Sage.

Roshell, S. (2016, June 7). The ugly secret of working moms. Cited in The Week.com.

Ropers-Huilman, B. (1998). Feminist leaders in higher education: A textual analysis of power and resistance. *Organization, 8,* 388–395.

Sallee, M. W. (2014). *Faculty fathers: Toward a new ideal in the research university.* Albany, NY: SUNY Press.

Sandberg, S. (2013). *Lean in: Women, work, and the will to lead.* New York, NY: Alfred A. Knopf.

Strauss, A., & Corbin, J. (1990). *Basics of qualitative research: Grounded theory procedures and techniques.* Newbury Park, CA: Sage.

Ward, K., & Wolf-Wendel, L. E. (2012) *Academic motherhood: Managing work and family.* New Brunswick, NJ: Rutgers University Press.

Weedon, C. (1996). *Feminist practice and poststructuralist theory.* Malden, MA: Blackwell.

KELLY WARD *is a professor of higher education and department chair at Washington State University.*

LISA WOLF-WENDEL *is a professor of higher education and Associate Dean for Research and Graduate Studies at the University of Kansas.*

NEW DIRECTIONS FOR HIGHER EDUCATION • DOI: 10.1002/he

2

This chapter explores how contingent faculty address the issue of work and family and demonstrates the importance of understanding the diversity of contingent faculty experiences and of underemployment rather than notions of the ideal worker to explain their work lives.

Contingent Faculty as Nonideal Workers

Adrianna Kezar, Samantha Bernstein-Sierra

Early on, I really appreciated the flexibility I had for years while I had young children. Not having to work full-time and being my own boss. But then as the children got older I wanted more challenge, and to be treated more like a professional, and to be paid fairly for the investment I was making. That's when being an adjunct wasn't great.

This quote from a non-tenure-track faculty member exemplifies the diverse and complex situation that contingent faculty members face as they try to combine their careers with their family. Research on part-time faculty (and full-time non-tenure-track faculty) often reflects the appeal of flexibility afforded by adjunct positions (Kezar & Sam, 2010). Many express the sentiment that when they were trying to meet family challenges, they found their workplace life fairly rewarding. When they had fewer family obligations, they often began to view their work lives differently and to see more downsides to contingent positions than they had seen initially.

In this chapter, we explore the diverse and complex experiences that contingent faculty members encounter as they try to navigate a career and family. As opposed to other groups reviewed in this volume, contingent faculty face fewer "ideal worker" struggles than tenure-track faculty and administrators. In order for the ideal worker norm to be relevant, the workers need to be visible to the institution. Institutions typically have no expectations for part-time faculty beyond teaching their courses (c.f., Ward, Morphew, & Wolf-Wendel, 2016). For this reason, their experiences can be explained more accurately by theories of underemployment.

In order to explore this topic, we begin by providing some background about contingent faculty members in higher education, particularly as it relates to the conundrum of women taking contingent faculty positions to

New Directions for Higher Education, no. 176, Winter 2016 © 2016 Wiley Periodicals, Inc.
Published online in Wiley Online Library (wileyonlinelibrary.com) • DOI: 10.1002/he.20207

balance family obligations based on the assumption that they will ultimately move into full-time or tenure-track positions. Unfortunately, data demonstrate that this hope is typically not realized (Schuster & Finkelstein, 2006). Following this background information, we describe research conducted with contingent faculty that explores their experiences, particularly noting some of the challenges and opportunities they describe when it comes to family and work-life balance. We conclude by considering the complicated qualitative data in light of the sobering and disappointing national data to consider future directions.

Background and Context

Non-tenure-track faculty (NTTF) or contingent faculty are those who are either part-time on term-to-term contracts or full-time on yearly or rolling contracts. What these faculty members share is a lack of job security. Part-time faculty currently comprise 52% of the faculty members in higher education, whereas full-time NTTF make up approximately 18% of the faculty (AFT Higher Education, 2010). To better understand the magnitude of this shift from tenure-track to contingent faculty, according to the most recent analyzed data, the total faculty in the United States number approximately 1.3 million and of those about 800,000 are non-tenure-track (AFT Higher Education, 2010). The part-time faculty category of employment continues to grow at the highest rate among all faculty members (Schuster & Finkelstein, 2006). But their experiences differ significantly from those of full-time contingent faculty, who often have working conditions, salary, and benefits similar to tenure-track faculty members and more diverse roles that sometimes include service, administration, and scholarship. Part-time faculty (often termed adjuncts) generally have very poor working conditions— low pay, no benefits, last-minute hiring, no mentoring or professional development, no involvement in curriculum planning or textbook choices, limited interaction with other faculty members, very little support from departmental staff, limited access to resources to support their teaching, and jobs defined almost exclusively by teaching (Kezar & Sam, 2010). Related to the focus of this volume, it is also important to note that contingent faculty often do not have access to family leave policies, particularly adjunct faculty who, as noted earlier, generally lack any access to benefits including on-campus child care (Kezar & Sam, 2010). Additionally, negative working conditions create special challenges for working mothers. For example, many contingent faculty have no office to use in order to nurse a child or use a breast pump. Full-time contingent faculty are more likely to have access to some of these family-friendly policies, but data suggest part-timers are much less likely to have such access (Kezar & Sam, 2010; Kezar, Maxey, & Holcombe, 2015).

We have very limited data about contingent faculty, and increasingly about tenure-track faculty as well, because national data are no longer being collected by the National Center for Education Statistics. Only recently have other faculty databases such as the Higher Education Research Institute faculty survey (http://heri.ucla.edu/facoverview.php) included any information on contingent or part-time faculty, and much of the data that are collected do not address issues such as responsibilities outside of work, particularly family life. Instead, the bulk of the available data on contingent faculty is obtained from qualitative research studies, small-scale quantitative studies, or single-institution studies. However, from existing data, we do know that contingent faculty are an extremely heterogeneous group and that describing any kind of representative for universal experience is quite difficult. Part-time faculty members might be retired tenure-track faculty or retired from other professions. They might be working artists who teach a few courses, full-time professionals in law or journalism, or aspiring academics who want full-time tenure-track positions. The fastest growing group is comprised of the aspiring academics (Coalition for the Academic Workforce [CAW], 2012).

An important distinction that has emerged in the research is whether these faculty work in the contingent status voluntarily or involuntarily. Those who are voluntary tend to be more satisfied with the role; whereas those who are involuntary are not only less satisfied, but also feel that they are underemployed (Kezar & Sam, 2010). Involuntary part-time faculty are least satisfied with their compensation, job security, and opportunities for advancement.

Qualitative studies point to the way contingent faculty worlds are multiple and divided between several units, fields, or communities—discipline, program, department, and the college or university. NTTFs sometimes teach in multiple fields, departments, and types of institutions so their experiences are much more complex than the usual faculty member who has a more singular and homogenous professional identity. Levin and Shaker (2011) studied full-time NTTF, noting: "[the] FTNTTF world is characterized by dissonance, where one set of values or norms is not congruent with another" (p. 13). This situation is likely even more complex for part-time NTTF who sometimes have other professional lives outside of academe. The majority of faculty in Levin and Shaker's (2011) study described themselves as possessing incoherent or conflictive identities: "They are divided selves, chameleon-like: they both accept and reject aspects of their professional roles and status; they live in the present but also in a future that is projected as better than the present" (p. 18). These few emerging studies on NTTF worldviews/experiences suggest that they are socially constructing their world in a complex and fragmented environment and that an understanding of this complexity is essential to better understanding, supporting, and integrating contingent faculty into the academy.

Various data points important to the topic of this chapter illustrate that women faculty are twice as likely as men to be contingent (Curtis, 2004; Schuster & Finkelstein, 2006). Wolfinger, Mason, and Goulden. (2009)

refer to the adjunct professorship as "the mommy track" because of its prevalence among women. In the NTTF Report (Association of American Universities [AAU], 2001), which looked at a sample of 30 AAU research universities, 45% of all NTTF were women. According to Forrest Cataldi, Fahimi, and Bradburn (2005), in 2003, 48% of part-time faculty were women and 52% were men. In contrast, in 2003, women only made up 38% of the tenure-track faculty. Perna (2001) found that women on contingent appointments tend to be married with children, demonstrating the overlap of family obligations with contingent employment. With women being overrepresented in the category of contingent faculty, they are often more likely to be dealing with work-life balance and family issues that continue to be the responsibility of women more so than men. Perna's research further identifies that women are trying to balance work and family, which is why they are so largely represented in the ranks of contingent faculty. Qualitative data suggest that women often take on part-time positions to be able to address family responsibilities (Bronstein, Rothblum, & Solomon, 1993).

Increasingly, various national studies focusing on science, technology, engineering, mathematics, and medicine have demonstrated the trend for women to take non-tenure-track positions to accommodate work-life balance (Curtis, 2004). Recent data suggest some further trends related to adjuncts and motherhood. Data from the research of Wolfinger et al. (2009) found that mothers with children under 6 years of age are much more likely to hold contingent roles and to remain in contingent positions. The data also suggest that these women are likely to leave the work force. For example, Wolfinger et al. (2009) note, "Women with children under six are much more likely than either men or other women to leave the labor force altogether. In contrast, older children substantially increase the chances of a mother's reentry into the academic workforce" (p. 1612). These reentry positions may be on the tenure track, though not necessarily. These researchers see the data point about reentry as a hopeful indicator that maybe there is a pathway back into work after taking time off and that leaving the faculty to raise children does not preclude a faculty career in the future—even a tenure-track one.

One of the challenges of taking on a part-time position while having a family with the hopes of transitioning to a full-time position later is that there is very little permeability between part-time and full-time positions in the academy. In examining national data sets, Schuster and Finkelstein (2006) found an "'exclusive' pattern of part-time employment for part-time faculty" (p. 208). They were surprised to find that so few part-timers ever moved into full-time employment and that there appeared to be a bias against hiring part-time faculty into full-time positions. Kezar's (2013a) work as a qualitative researcher supports the contention that hiring committees are not favorable to considering part-timers at their own institutions for full-time positions.

New Directions for Higher Education • DOI: 10.1002/he

This background provides an understanding of what contingent positions are like, how they have grown in recent years, and who contingent faculty are, including the representation of women in this sector who are often trying to balance family responsibilities. One of the most disheartening data points is the limited permeability that exists between part-time and full-time work, and it is one of the primary reasons that women become trapped in extremely poor work situations that offer them limited opportunities for advancement.

Being Catalyzed into Part-Time Positions to Support Family: Underemployment

One of the major challenges of being a part-time faculty member is that there is no designated track for career advancement. Part-timers become stuck in a cycle of term-to-term employment with no opportunities for new challenges, mentoring, feedback, or ways to become engaged and involved with their campus (Kezar & Sam, 2010).

While balancing family, NTTF frequently forgo salary and benefits, particularly if they have a spouse or partner who can compensate for the lower income. The average salary for part-time faculty is $3,000 per course, which typically means that their salary would max out at approximately $24,000 a year with a full-time course load (CAW, 2012). Over time, the low salary, lack of benefits, and job insecurity make the position extremely difficult, despite its potential advantages in accommodating families. After an approximately 5-year period of focusing on family, NTTF are locked into a lifetime of second-class status, often becoming resentful and unsatisfied (Kezar, 2013a).

Theories of underemployment are helpful for explaining the experience of contingent faculty members with families. Underemployment is the condition in which employees believe that their skills and talents are not being effectively utilized in the workplace (Maynard & Joseph, 2008). When individuals are underemployed, this tends to relate to a series of negative outcomes including low morale, turnover, dissatisfaction, absenteeism, and, over time, lower performance.

Underemployment explains the situation when, as noted earlier, women are interested in, but unable to transition into full-time roles from part-time positions (Maynard & Joseph, 2008). In addition, even those in full-time non-tenure-track positions often find themselves underemployed because the institution may not include them in governance, decision-making, or the broader professional life of the campus (Ward et al., 2016). Therefore, both part-time and full-time contingent faculty often find themselves in conditions of underemployment.

There are some situations in which ideal worker norms may be applied to contingent faculty members. At some institutions, for example, pressures are created for part-time faculty to do additional service work or work beyond teaching their courses in order to meet departmental needs, and this work is typically uncompensated (Ward et al., 2016). Departments create pressure for part-time faculty by suggesting that if a full-time position were to open, only those part-timers who have contributed additional service time will be eligible or looked upon favorably for these positions. As noted earlier, very few part-timers are ever hired to be full-time at their institutions. However, the possibility of moving to full-time employment—however remote—often results in a juggling act of additional work, unpaid work obligations, and sacrificing family time in the hopes of moving out of underemployment.

Kezar's (2013b) and Shaker's (2008) research also suggests that ideal worker norms drive contingent faculty members to put in many additional hours beyond what they are paid in order to fulfill their obligation of how they define a quality professor, which was developed through their training in graduate school. This is not unexpected given the fact that contingent faculty have the same socialization and training as tenure-track faculty members and, for example, feel the same need to keep up on the scholarship in their field even though they are not being paid to do so. Therefore, although the institution may not hold specific expectations for contingent faculty to keep up on scholarship, publishing, and research, update their teaching on an ongoing basis, engage in professional or national service, spend additional time with students, and develop professionally, contingent faculty often hold themselves to the ideal worker norms based on their graduate school socialization. Additionally, one could imagine contingent faculty hold themselves to ideal teacher norms since their main role is teaching and they are committed to their careers and work additional unpaid hours in support of students. The lack of support in terms of technology, staff, resources, office space, and low compensation makes it extremely difficult to meet this ideal teaching norm. Although we have very limited research currently on this issue, it is an area that is important for continued examination and suggests that ideal worker norms may play a larger role in the lives of contingent faculty than we currently understand.

Balancing Work and Family

Studies examining the experience of contingent faculty have identified the flexibility of part-time employment as one of the sources of satisfaction for many individuals in this role, particularly to accommodate family (Kezar & Sam, 2010; Waltman Bergom, Hollenshead, Miller, & August, 2012). This finding emerged in studies by Gappa (1984) and continues to be found in more recent studies (Waltman et al., 2012). Flexibility and time to address family obligations are consistently mentioned as important advantages of part-time positions. Additionally, participants in these studies mentioned being relieved of the pressures of tenure and the stress of departmental and university politics. They appreciate the ability to work with students and to teach courses but also to be unencumbered by many other institutional responsibilities they found less interesting.

Studies also reinforce that, although there are sources of satisfaction from part-time and contingent positions, faculty members experience the frustration that comes with a lack of promotional opportunities, limited professional development, and very unclear expectations about contribution and organizational citizenship (Kezar, 2013a). NTTF also register many other sources of dissatisfaction, such as low salary, lack of benefits, job security, second-class citizenship, and disrespect. Thus, NTTF who choose contingent status in order to better balance work and family often end up sacrificing opportunities and full-time professional life in exchange for flexibility.

One of the few studies that directly examine gender issues related to NTTF developed a similar finding to Levin and Shaker (2011) about the fragmented and complex narratives of women faculty off the tenure track (Hart, 2011). Before the study, Hart anticipated that she would hear more uniformly marginalized or equity-oriented stories. However, the work climate for NTTF was disparate, and they experienced their work lives in different ways, depending on the department in which they were housed, changes that occurred over time within the department, and their own changing and emerging views about equity or marginalization. Women NTTF described how their context and experiences created an incoherent and fragmented environment—neither marginalization nor equity were constants. Instead, conditions changed based on new department chairs, turnovers in leadership, relationships, and their own changing perspectives.

Kezar's (2013b) own research with contingent faculty reinforces these findings about complexity. She found that contingent faculty do not universally find part-time work either demeaning or beneficial while they balance their family lives. Not all NTTF experience underemployment but, over the course of their careers, many do. Individual life conditions such as career stage and organizational features such as history of the department shape the way NTTF construct support at any given time, and this process of constructing work-life balance is dynamic and changing over a career. Among the variety of individual and organizational issues that shape the complex and fragmented reality of contingent faculty, one of the areas Kezar (2013b) has examined is life phase, where issues of work-life balance are particularly prevalent.

In this research, women faculty members who had children felt that their departments were supportive when they were caring for children, even if the department lacked the characteristics in the literature that are noted as important to support faculty performance such as professional development, benefits, job security, or involvement in governance and curriculum (Kezar, 2013b). NTTF women faculty (more often those who were married) thought of support quite differently when they had family as priority. One woman faculty member spoke about this issue:

NEW DIRECTIONS FOR HIGHER EDUCATION • DOI: 10.1002/he

> I felt the department was supportive for a long time because I was bringing up our children and so the lack of job security and second class treatment just mattered less to me then. But now my children have grown up and it's as if I see the department differently now, and I recognize that I'm not treated as a professional and this isn't a supportive environment and now I want to go someplace else.

Although care for children was brought up most often, faculty also described caring for elderly or sick family members. The general pattern of caregiving made an individual less focused on departmental supports.

Consistently, though, faculty members changed their views as their priorities shifted over their life (Kezar, 2013b). The poor working conditions, lack of support, and underemployment were not sustainable, and NTTF talked about how they saw many aspiring faculty members change careers after 5 years of teaching. Five years was usually the point at which NTTF began to see that the lack of support was not a passing phase, but a permanent aspect of their career that would have a long-lasting effect on their opportunities as a professional (Kezar, 2013b). As one woman explained:

> I think early career faculty just do not think about how the department will impact them, they feel autonomous, but then they have three or four bad experiences with other colleagues, of losing all classes for a semester and being without income, or have a health scare and then they realize this is not going to be something they can continue, no matter how much they love teaching.

Another faculty member spoke to the issue of underemployment:

> I was just so happy to be teaching and feel like I was using my degree. But as my kids went into school, I started to look at my work in different ways. I realized I did not have any professional interaction, there is no support in my department for going to conferences or for professional development, and now I started to have time and want to do these things and there just isn't any possibility or opportunity. So, as I said, I was happy for a while, but then things changed.

It is important not to see colleagues as static and instead recognize that their needs for support may change over time. For example, faculty members in the phase of life after raising their children or as children get older are likely to have different needs than those who are raising young children. Although this is true for tenure-track faculty as well, the fragmentation of NTTF careers means that their pathways are more dynamic than what one would expect for a typical tenure-track faculty member.

Chairs need to be aware of the changing needs and support of NTTFs. The details of their career trajectory are often overlooked by those creating policies and practices. Also, NTTF may not feel underemployed at one point in time, but because this may change as they have fewer family obligations, chairs and other academic leaders should have specific times when they can systematically check in with faculty to identify their need for greater challenges or availability for additional involvement.

National Data and Local Stories: A Future

Research suggests that women move into adjunct and contingent positions that are satisfying for some period of time but then become trapped in these positions which become less desirable as they begin to feel underemployed (Kezar, 2013b). Although the situation is more prevalent for women, it is also occurring among men who accept contingent positions, and as a result, many qualified and strong faculty members end up leaving the academy. As an enterprise, we can certainly do better to create roles where faculty members can have flexibility for a time but also move into more professionally rewarding careers as their outside responsibilities change. We offer up a set of recommendations that can help colleges and universities in their support of NTTF.

One of the best ways to address this issue is to create more career mobility between adjunct and full-time positions. We need to make hiring committees aware of their bias and failure to consider their own strong part-time candidates for full-time positions. We need to draw attention to the importance of hiring the faculty who are already familiar with students at the institution, the learning objectives of the program, and the culture. There is a strong bias to hire national candidates rather than seek out local talent.

Another way to address this issue is to provide professional advancement for part-time faculty. Some institutions are exploring the possibility of promotional tracks for part-time faculty members so that they can move up the ranks from assistant, associate, to full professor and have more opportunities for professional development funds, involvement in decision-making, and opportunities for leadership over the course of their career. Some institutions have long had different titles for part-time faculty who come in with different expertise (e.g., professors of practice). What is occurring now is more than just a difference in titles among part-time faculty but a true professional track where these individuals go through evaluation and feedback processes and have opportunities for salary increases and other professional perks.

Additionally, improving the working conditions for part-time faculty would address the needs of those who are unable to move from part-time to full-time employment. Although creating a promotional track within the part-time faculty is one way to improve their overall working conditions, ensuring that part-time faculty at any promotional rank have access to mentoring and professional feedback is important. And, of course, one of the areas that has not been addressed and is important to work-life balance for

NEW DIRECTIONS FOR HIGHER EDUCATION • DOI: 10.1002/he

contingent faculty is creating specific policies that support their balancing of work and life such as paid leave, access to child care, shared office space for working parents, and other important policies that would support contingent faculty who are mothers and fathers. We know tenure-track faculty often hesitate to utilize work-life balance policies for fear it will impact their careers—not being seen as a serious scholar if they take time off, for example. It is likely these concerns will be even greater among contingent faculty whose lives are so precarious. Kezar et.al (2015) and Kezar and Sam (2010) have called for longer-term and multiyear contracts to help support issues like academic freedom and involvement in shared governance, but this will also support utilization of work-life balance policies. Through the development of longer-term contracts and as faculty do not fear that their role is in jeopardy each term, they are more likely to feel comfortable utilizing work-life balance policies. There are many important changes that can be made to improve part-time faculty work lives, and further recommendations can be obtained from the Delphi projects on the changing faculty and student success: www.thechangingfaculty.org.

Kezar's (2013b) research also points out that contingent faculty themselves also have a wealth of ideas about ways to create a more supportive environment from comparisons they have made between departments or institutions, since they often work across several institutions, or from discussions, they have had with colleagues that highlight common challenges. None of the faculty she interviewed had ever been asked for ideas about improving the support or climate for the department. It seems that, to date, colleges and universities have missed the opportunity to tap into contingent faculty expertise in finding ways to help them create work-life balance, to address underemployment, and, in general, to provide better support for them in their professional lives.

References

Association of American Universities. (2001). *Non-tenure-track faculty report*. Retrieved from https://www.aau.edu/WorkArea/DownloadAsset.aspx?id=466

AFT Higher Education. (2010). A national survey of part-time/adjunct faculty. *American Academic, 2,* 1–15.

Bronstein, P., Rothblum, E. D., & Solomon, S. E. (1993). Ivy halls and glass walls: Barriers to academic careers for women and ethnic minorities. In J. Gainen & R. Boice (Eds.), *New directions for teaching and learning: No. 53. Building a diverse faculty* (pp. 17–31) San Francisco, CA: Jossey-Bass.

Coalition for the Academic Workforce (CAW). (2012). *A portrait of part-time faculty members: A summary of findings on part-time faculty respondents to the Coalition on the Academic Workforce Survey of Contingent Faculty Members and Instructors*. Retrieved from http://www.academicworkforce.org/CAW_portrait_2012.pdf

Curtis, J. W. (2004). Balancing work and family for faculty: Why it's important. *Academe, 90*(6), 21.

Forrest Cataldi, E., Fahimi, M., & Bradburn, E. M. (2005). *National Study of Postsecondary Faculty (NSOPF: 04) Report on faculty and instructional staff in fall 2003* (NCES

2005-172). Washington, DC: U.S. Department of Education, National Center for Education Statistics, 1993–1994.

Gappa, J. M. (1984). Part-time faculty: Higher education at a crossroads. *ASHE-ERIC Higher Education Research Report, 3*. Washington, DC: Association for the Study of Higher Education.

Hart, J. (2011). Non-tenure track women faculty: Opening the door. *Journal of the Professoriate, 4*(1), 96–124.

Kezar, A. (2013a). Four cultures of the new academy: Support for non-tenure-track faculty. *The Journal of Higher Education, 84*(2), 153–158.

Kezar, A. (2013b). Non-tenure-track faculty's social construction of a supportive work environment. *Teachers College Record, 115*(12), n12.

Kezar, A., Maxey, D., & Holcombe, E. (2015). *The professoriate reconsidered: Stakeholder views of new faculty models*. New York, NY: TIAA-CREF Research Institute.

Kezar, A., & Sam, C. (2010). Understanding the new majority of non-tenure-track faculty in higher education—demographics, experiences, and plans of action. *ASHE Higher Education Report, 36*(4).

Levin, J. S., & Shaker, G. G. (2011). The hybrid and dualistic identity of full-time non-tenure-track faculty. *American Behavioral Scientist, 55*(11), 1461–1484.

Maynard, D. C., & Joseph, T. A. (2008). Are all part-time faculty underemployed? The influence of faculty status preference on satisfaction and commitment. *Higher Education, 55*(2), 139–154.

Perna, L. W. (2001). The relationship between family responsibilities and employment status among college and university faculty. *The Journal of Higher Education, 72*, 584–611.

Schuster, J. H., & Finkelstein, M. J. (2006). *The American faculty: The restructuring of academic work and careers*. Baltimore, MD: Johns Hopkins University Press.

Shaker, G. (2008). *Off the track: The full-time non-tenure-track faculty experience in English* (Unpublished doctoral dissertation, Indiana University, Bloomington, IN).

Waltman, J., Bergom, I., Hollenshead, C., Miller, J., & August, L. (2012). Factors contributing to job satisfaction and dissatisfaction among non-tenure-track faculty. *The Journal of Higher Education, 83*(3), 411–434.

Ward, K., Morphew, C., & Wolf-Wendel, L. (2016). *Faculty roles and expectations*. Council of Independent Colleges Report, Washington, DC.

Wolfinger, N. H., Mason, M. A., & Goulden, M. (2009). Stay in the game: Gender, family formation and alternative trajectories in the academic life course. *Social Forces, 87*(3), 1591–1621.

ADRIANNA KEZAR *is professor for higher education at the University of Southern California and co-director of the Pullias Center for Higher Education.*

SAMANTHA BERNSTEIN-SIERRA *is a PhD candidate of urban education policy at the University of Southern California's Rossier School of Education.*

NEW DIRECTIONS FOR HIGHER EDUCATION • DOI: 10.1002/he

3

This chapter explores the work-life experiences of administrators as well as whether and how the ideal worker model affects those experiences. Departmental and supervisory differences and technology complicate administrators' work-life experiences.

Work-Life Balance and Ideal Worker Expectations for Administrators

Kelly E. Wilk

Work-life balance is a well-documented problem for employees in corporate America (e.g., Harrington, Van Deusen, & Ladge, 2010; Matos & Galinsky, 2011), but the academy has been much slower to realize the benefits of developing a work-life-friendly culture (Anderson, Morgan, & Wilson, 2002). Studies on work-life in the academy tend to focus on faculty members and how workplace norms pressure faculty to conform to the ideal worker model (Grant, Kennelly, & Ward, 2000; Rice, Sorcinelli, & Austin, 2000; Thompson, 2008). In response, many universities have implemented work-life policies to improve the work experience for faculty (Finkel & Olswang, 1996; Mason & Goulden, 2004; Sallee, 2012).

Nonfaculty employees comprise nearly half of the academy's workforce (Rhoades, 2007). Yet, few studies focus solely on nonfaculty employees (Anderson et al., 2002; Herman & Gyllstrom, 1977). The present study focuses on administrators in higher education. Administrators play an important role in the work of the academy, performing much of the planning, decision-making, and goal-setting for their institutions. What are the work-life balance experiences of administrators in the academy? Do administrators, like faculty, experience pressure to conform to the ideal worker model? This study explores how administrators' understanding of workplace norms and ideal worker expectations affected their work-life experience and behavior at a doctoral-granting institution. Understanding how this population manages work-life expectations could have important implications for productivity, retention, and the development of a more equitable work environment in the academy.

New Directions for Higher Education, no. 176, Winter 2016   © 2016 Wiley Periodicals, Inc.
Published online in Wiley Online Library (wileyonlinelibrary.com) • DOI: 10.1002/he.20208

Who Is an Administrator?

Administrators are present in the president's office, student affairs, athletics, development, academic departments, and other areas. Administrators are responsible for addressing students' noninstructional needs, engaging in day-to-day problem solving, and facilitating long-term institutional planning. It is useful to divide nonfaculty employees into two groups: administrators and staff. Studies that combine these two groups of nonfaculty employees together (e.g., Gillespie, Walsh, Winefield, Dua, & Stough, 2001; Winefield et al., 2003) conflate the experiences of these employees who occupy fundamentally different jobs.

In this study, I define an administrator as someone whose position is exempt or salaried under the Fair Labor Standards Act (FLSA). The FLSA requires employers to classify their employees' positions into two groups: exempt from overtime and not exempt from overtime. In order for a position to be classified as exempt, or salaried, the position must have a significant level of discretion and responsibility for making independent judgments. Exempt employees are not compensated if they work more than the standard number of full-time hours per week designated by the institution; they are expected to do what is necessary to accomplish their work. Exempt employees also have responsibility for more of the professional, strategic work of the institution.

What We Know About Administrators' Work-Life Experiences

Administrators comprise a growing segment of professionals on college and university campuses and, at some institutions, administrators outnumber faculty members (Rhoades & Sporn, 2002). Despite the rise of administrators on campuses, work-life research on this group of employees is limited. Bailey (2008) conducted qualitative interviews with nine occupational deans at community colleges in the Midwest to understand how they managed their work and personal lives, the issues that they faced, and whether they struggled to manage their multiple roles. Many of the deans reported tension between their personal and professional lives. The study's findings are limited due to the small pool of participants and the representation of only one level of administration.

Other researchers have studied work-life balance for nonfaculty employees but have done so with more of a psychological focus on job stress and strain. Winefield et al. (2003) surveyed 9,732 employees at 17 Australian universities and found that academic staff showed greater levels of psychological strain and lower levels of job satisfaction than general staff. All the participants in Gillespie et al.'s (2001) study indicated that stress in the workplace had affected them both personally and professionally, and half of the participants described sacrificing time with their families in order to meet job expectations. These studies have limited applicability to U.S. higher education, but they do indicate that stress in the workplace affects work-life balance for administrators. They suggest the need for studies of college administrators to be conducted in the U.S. context.

The Ideal Worker Model

Many studies of employees' work-life experiences have utilized the conceptual framework of the ideal worker model. The ideal worker is present in the workplace and logs the requisite face-time hours needed during regular work hours and beyond. This study defines face time as the amount of interaction between employees and their supervisors and coworkers, as well as the amount of time that an employee is present in the office (Elsbach, Cable, & Sherman, 2010). Today's workplace is still organized around the ideal of a worker for whom employment is the only responsibility in his or her life (Bailyn, 1993; Bailyn, Drago, & Kochan, 2001). The image of the ideal worker is framed around typical male life patterns of decades past in which men worked outside of the home while women handled household and familial responsibilities (Williams, 2000). Although such arrangements were more common in previous decades, they are unrealistic in today's dual-career environment.

Purpose of the Study

This qualitative study examines whether and how workplace norms and ideal worker expectations affect the work-life balance experiences of college administrators. Workplace norms were defined as the behaviors endorsed by the culture of the organization (Bess & Dee, 2008). Casper, Eby, Bordeaux, Lockwood, & Lambert (2007) suggested that work-life research needs to move beyond the individual level to a greater examination of work-life at the group, department, or organizational level. To assess how workplace norms regarding work-life balance differed for administrators across one institution, I solicited participation from two very different groups of administrators—those who worked in the Division of Technology (referred to as Technology) and those who worked in the Division of Student Affairs (referred to as Student Affairs). Both groups work at the same private, doctoral-granting institution.

Findings from research on the corporate world show that employees often feel compelled to conform to the expectations of the ideal worker model, which impacts the ways in which they experience work-life balance (Bailyn, 1993; Thompson, 2008; Williams, 2000). I included administrators who worked in Technology at the university in this study because those workers occupied positions that are comparable to those in the corporate world. For example, the job responsibilities of a systems administrator are similar regardless of whether that individual works in the academy or in the corporate world. In contrast, student affairs professionals face different job demands based on the student-oriented nature of their positions. Student affairs administrators work in positions that are unique to higher education;

NEW DIRECTIONS FOR HIGHER EDUCATION • DOI: 10.1002/he

their positions rarely exist in organizations outside of the academy (Winston, Creamer, & Miller, 2001). Student Affairs administrators in this study worked in student housing, academic advising, career and personal counseling, and student activities. As previous researchers have found, these administrators often have to make themselves available to students by working evening and weekend hours (Forney, Wallace-Schutzman, & Wiggers, 1982; Lorden, 1998).

The very different jobs and workplace contexts for administrators in Technology and in Student Affairs enabled me to explore how administrators with jobs that were similar to those in the corporate world fared in terms of their work-life balance, and how administrators with student-oriented jobs that were unique to higher education experienced work-life balance in the academy. Through these two groups of participants, I investigated how administrators understood work-life balance at one institution, how their understanding of workplace norms and ideal worker expectations affected their work-life balance experience and behavior, and how their experiences and understanding compared and contrasted by division and department.

Methods

I recruited participants from the population of administrators at a private, 4-year institution in the Northeast that, for the purposes of this study, I named Plains University. Rhoades (2007) noted that across the higher-education literature, there is a dearth of information on nonelite 4-year schools including public comprehensive colleges and universities and private liberal arts institutions. The same is true of the work-life balance segment of the higher-education literature; most researchers have focused on the experiences of faculty at research institutions.

Semistructured, in-depth interviews were conducted with 25 male and female administrators who were between the ages of 25 and 60 and had worked at the university for at least 2 years. I conducted interviews until additional data no longer enhanced the categories that I had developed and the data reached the point of saturation. Data analysis was a continuous, reflective activity that occurred throughout the writing process and consisted of both within case and cross-case analysis. Several measures were taken to ensure the validity of the study's findings including transcription checks, follow up with participants, and member reflections, which help to mitigate observer effects in analysis and writing (LeCompte & Goetz, 2007; Tracy, 2010).

Findings

The area in which an administrator worked at Plains affected both the administrator's work-life balance experience and his or her perception of the ideal worker. Although a part of the larger university, each division had its own culture, expectations, and accepted practices. Although I intended to compare and contrast ideal worker norms in Student Affairs and in Technology, I found there were two very different work environments in the IT technical area and in the IT creative area. Administrators in the IT creative area performed work related to website design and instructional technology. Administrators in the IT technical area handled programming, systems, and networking. They were responsible for maintaining Plains University's technological systems and ensuring that they functioned smoothly.

Student Affairs Administrators.   Previous research has documented the long hours that student affairs administrators typically work (Forney et al., 1982; Lorden, 1998). The Student Affairs administrators in this study were no exception. Administrators in Student Affairs experienced face-time pressure to be present during the university's regular business hours and beyond. Sally shared, "My supervisor's supervisor has made it very clear to me that I'm expected to be here nine to five." Joy stated that her supervisor felt "very strongly about the office always being manned" during the workday.

Although administrators felt that their presence was expected in the office during regular business hours, working evening and weekend hours also was the norm in Student Affairs. Twelve of the 14 Student Affairs administrators reported that they regularly worked evening and weekend hours. Several administrators indicated that to expect to resolve students' problems within a nine-to-five timeframe was unrealistic since students were on campus 24 hours a day, 7 days a week.

Even though many of the Student Affairs administrators felt pressure to be present during the workday and for evening and weekend activities, all of them reported that they had some degree of flexibility. Most of the administrators had a supervisor who enabled them to flex their hours when necessary in order to accommodate stretches of long hours and/or late nights. Despite the flexibility that the Student Affairs supervisors offered to their administrators, more than half of the administrators were not satisfied with their overall work-life balance, and 79% admitted that they had difficulty finding a balance between their personal and professional lives.

Administrators knew that their supervisors expected them to be present during regular business hours, but they and their supervisors also acknowledged that their jobs could not be fully accomplished within regular business hours. This led to confusion on the part of the administrators. They imposed evening and weekend hours on themselves but were not entirely certain how many evening and weekend hours they needed to work in order to be successful in their jobs or to appear as ideal workers. In order to offset the sometimes difficult schedules that their employees worked, supervisors provided administrators with opportunities to come into work late, to take a day off, or to leave early. Although this kept the administrators relatively happy, they also acknowledged the impact that their jobs had on their personal lives.

Informal flexibility made some administrators feel that coming in late or leaving early was not officially condoned, and they were, therefore, sometimes hesitant to take advantage of such opportunities. Administrators also knew that they were expected to be present during the workday and to log the face-time hours. The supervisors in Student Affairs sent mixed messages to administrators about the ideal worker. The established culture of working long hours further added to administrators' pressure to be present during the regular workday and after hours. Supervisory face-time expectations and the culture of working long hours left many of the Student Affairs administrators feeling discontent with their work-life balance.

IT Technical Administrators.   Those who worked in the IT technical area were the most likely to talk about pressure to maintain a physical presence in the office. Regardless of job title, all of them described pressure to report on time for work and to be present during the university's regular nine-to-five business hours. According to Felicia, a young mother, the ideal worker in the IT technical area is always present during business hours. "At Plains University, you're expected to be on time and to stay throughout the day." She described the pressure on time and presence as "not very family-friendly."

Nearly everyone in the IT technical area reported that they were unable to telecommute. According to Jonathan, "an expectation in IT, here, is that you can't work mobilely [sic]. This is the only IT position I've ever been in where that was the mindset. That's the culture." Administrators were rarely offered accommodations like flexible hours or telecommuting, and if they were, they were hesitant to take advantage of them because of the emphasis on physical presence at work during business hours.

Like the administrators in Student Affairs, three-quarters of the IT technical administrators talked about working long hours, evenings, and weekends. Out of all the administrators in Technology, IT technical administrators were the most likely to report that their jobs made demands on their time 24/7. Nico shared that he was "always connected," and Raul reported receiving late night calls and that he always kept his work phone close to him. "I don't think it's ever further than 10 feet away."

The majority of the IT technical administrators worked evening and weekend hours, in large part, due to the 24/7 demands of their work and expectations that all systems would always be available. Unlike Student Affairs, there was no culture of flexibility supported by the IT technical area. IT technical administrators desired to be able to telecommute and to adopt the flexible work practices of many of their peers who worked in IT at other organizations. There was a very different atmosphere, however, in the IT creative area.

IT Creative Administrators.   Although most IT creative administrators were expected to work during the university's regular business hours, there was a much more flexible culture in the IT creative environment than in the IT technical area or in Student Affairs. The supervisors in the IT creative area focused heavily on work results over physical presence, so administrators were able to flex their hours and/or telecommute. IT creative administrators indicated that their jobs made demands on their time but did not describe the 24/7 pressure that the IT technical employees described. IT creative administrators also reported little face-time pressure. Instead, these administrators described a far more flexible work environment in which telecommuting was permitted and accepted than the IT technical administrators. Bob stated, "I have a lot of flexibility" and noted that his supervisor was very understanding, "he gets it."

Much of this flexibility stemmed from the attitudes of the supervisors toward work. Marty noted,

> I've always thought that my role as a manager is to make sure that I make the work environment as good as I possibly can. I try to kick my employees out at five o'clock every day, no matter what's going on. Most of the time, I don't even have to kick them out. They know the expectation is "it's five o'clock, I should go."

Marty, like his supervisor, focused on results: "The way I've always looked at it, and the way I know my boss looks at it with me, is as long as your work's getting done."

IT creative administrators had far more flexibility to manage their lives at work and their lives outside of work than IT technical administrators. IT creative administrators were able to telecommute or to work a flexible schedule. The ideal worker in the IT creative area produced sound results on a reliable basis. He was regularly present at work but had the flexibility to telecommute or to flex his hours when needed. Telecommuting and working flexible hours were an established part of the culture in the IT creative area and were endorsed by the supervisors. Administrators appreciated this work environment; all of the administrators rated their overall work-life balance as excellent or good.

The Complicating Effect of Technology.   Although ideal worker norms varied in the three work areas at Plains, technology unilaterally blurred the lines between personal and professional life for administrators. In a study of 483 professionals, managers, and executives, Deal (2013) found that 60% used a smartphone for business work between 13.5 and 18.5 hours per day. Employees are increasingly unable to disengage with work after business hours as technology blurs the lines between work and nonwork (Deal, 2013; Grotto, 2015; Kossek, in press).

In this study, technology complicated administrators' work-life experiences and interpretations of the ideal worker. Administrators mentioned the ways in which technology had altered the workplace and their ability to balance work with responsibilities outside of work. Boundaries that once separated work from other aspects of administrators' lives have disappeared as technology has made working around the clock possible (Currie & Eveline, 2011; Deal, 2013; Kossek, in press). Administrators acknowledged that they checked email and responded to phone calls and text messages on evenings, weekends, vacations, and sick days. Technology placed pressure on administrators in two ways. First, the existence and the availability of technology gave administrators pressure to engage with the workplace beyond regular business hours or while they were away from the office. Some saw the ability to always be connected positively while others believed that it was problematic. Second, because they could always be connected, 40% of administrators used technology as a strategy to avoid being crushed by email when they returned to the office following a weekend or a day off. This tactic, however, had consequences for their personal lives.

Technology enabled administrators to maintain a connection to work whenever, wherever. Most administrators, however, believed that the rapid response time expectations imposed by technology and the ability to always be connected placed pressure on them while they were at work and while they were away from work. Maria described the ways in which technology had changed students' expectations in terms of response time from her office.

> The student will send an email to us, or they'll post something on the Plains University Facebook page, and if we don't respond in three minutes, they call. So there is an expectation of 24/7 accessibility on the part of some of our students and their family members because of the way technology now drives our world.

The ability to always be connected left some administrators feeling as though they did, in fact, always have to be connected. They felt that their supervisors and coworkers expected them to respond to calls, text messages, and emails on their personal devices during vacation and sick days. Maggie shared,

> The way we use technology today has changed the workforce noticeably from a nine-to-five kind of thing. I have my cell phone with me all of the time. It sleeps next to me because in this job, I do get phone calls in the middle of the night. So, in a real way, we are chained to our work.

Nadine vented about text messages from her colleagues or her supervisor that apologized for contacting her while she was on vacation but requested a response. Phil deliberately booked vacations that would take him "off the grid" and render him inaccessible to his coworkers. Around the clock connectivity gave administrators at all levels and in all areas pressure to remain connected and to engage. Many developed different strategies to cope with this pressure. Some administrators gave into the pressure and responded to phone calls and text messages; others devised ways to make themselves inaccessible from time to time.

Forty percent of all administrators reported that they responded to email after hours and on the weekends because they wanted to save themselves from more work when they returned to the office. Jacob referred to the ability to check emails from home as the "double-edged sword" of technology. "Even if I take a sick day, I'll probably open up my laptop and do some work just because you don't want emails to pile up." Although some administrators caved into the pressure of responding to technology around the clock with the intention of easing their workload, they found that they did so at the expense of introducing their jobs to their lives outside of the workplace. Maria shared, "I responded to my first email this morning at 6:30, before I said 'good morning' to my husband who was lying in bed next to me." Joy explained,

> My son made a comment the other day. He said, "Mommy's always texting" and I said, "I'm not always texting. There are other things that I do on my phone besides texting" and now I'm aware of it. I watch myself. If I'm around him, I try not to get on my phone as often.

This strategy of keeping up with email in order to manage one's work caused work to spill over into administrators' personal lives.

Technology has created new pressure for administrators to be connected and driven them to devise new ways to manage their work, like checking email on days off and on weekends. For some, this pressure was self-imposed as administrators strove to respond to students, supervisors, and colleagues. Others felt that their supervisors expected them to respond because they could always be connected to the workplace. Workplace expectations surrounding technology and response time are often murky (Deal, 2013). Thus, in the absence of clear guidelines, administrators may impose expectations upon themselves to respond to technology around the clock to ease their own workload. They also may believe that their supervisors have an expectation that they will answer after-hours phone calls, texts, and emails; in other words, they have been led to believe that the ideal worker is always connected and responsive. Technology has caused work to spill over into administrators' lives outside of the workplace and blurred the lines that separate when work ends and life outside of the workplace begins.

Discussion

As previous research has shown, supervisors play a key role in employees' work-life balance experiences (Allen, 2008; Clark, 2000; Grant et al., 2000;

Jo, 2008; Sallee, 2013). Plains University was no exception. With few formal work-life policies at the university, supervisors drove the culture and the practices surrounding administrators' flexibility and consequently, work-life balance experiences and perceptions of the ideal worker.

Although supervisor-driven flexibility was helpful for some Plains administrators, the university's supervisor-driven atmosphere regarding flexibility led to unequal experiences for administrators who worked in different areas, especially those who worked in the Division of Technology. Allison confirmed that, "across the entire IT organization, flexibility is not equal." While several of the IT administrators whom I interviewed mentioned the IT technical area's resistance to flexibility, most attributed it to management or to leadership. Only one IT technical supervisor offered a possible explanation for the resistance: top leadership's preference for management by "walking around." Thus, IT technical administrators might have been more liable to experience face-time pressure because their division was housed in the same building as the top leadership of the Division of Technology. Since the IT creative administrators worked in a separate building, they may have been shielded from some of the face-time pressure that their IT technical colleagues experienced. It is also possible, however, that the IT creative leaders were more willing to defy the established face-time expectation in the division than their IT technical colleagues.

Researchers have documented that supervisor-driven flexibility leads to different outcomes for different employees (Jo, 2008). Rappoport, Bailyn, Fletcher, and Pruitt (2002) found that individually negotiated solutions in the workplace helped individuals to balance but had little impact on the underlying culture in the workplace. Although Student Affairs administrators were offered informal practices that helped them to maintain a sense of balance on occasion, the culture and ideal worker norms (i.e., long hours and a physical presence at evening and weekend events) were at odds with this flexibility. In contrast, although the culture of the IT creative area supported work-life flexibility, administrators still felt pressure to report to work during regular business hours and to be cautious about how frequently they requested accommodations.

Administrators in all three work areas revealed that technology has created new challenges and expectations with regard to balancing life at work with life outside of the workplace. Feelings about work or work experiences carry or spill over into an individual's life outside of work; likewise, events outside of work can spill over into the workplace and impact one's performance at work (Barnett, 1998; Clark, 2000; Sorcinelli & Near, 1989). Evidence in support of spillover theory challenges the notion that work and life outside of work can be organized into tidy separate spheres, an important component of the ideal worker model. Instead, individuals hold multiple roles that influence each other (Barnett, 1998). Technology has increasingly blurred and complicated the overlapping nature of the multiple roles held by the Plains administrators. Consequently, administrators were usually unclear about when and how often they needed to use technology in order to remain connected to the workplace.

According to the ideal worker model, the productivity and commitment of an employee is judged by the total hours that the employee spends at the workplace (Hewlett, 2007; Thompson, 2008). Face time is an important component of the ideal worker model, but technology has complicated the traditional concept of the ideal worker since work is no longer limited to the physical office. Grotto (2015) suggested that today's technological changes have created jobs that require constant availability. Although employee productivity and commitment historically was judged, and in some workplaces continues to be judged, based on face time at work, technology has morphed physical face-time expectations into 24/7 connectivity expectations. The varied, unclear expectations surrounding technology and connectivity left administrators in this study confused and dissatisfied.

Administrators appreciated the ability to be constantly connected, but many specifically stated that they desired guidance around when and how to use technology in order to remain connected to the workplace. Across both divisions, administrators desired formal work-life policies, even those who worked in areas where flexible accommodations were offered on an informal basis. Without formal policies, administrators worried that they were not performing as ideal workers when they took advantage of informal flexible accommodations.

The importance of having written, accessible, and detailed policies about work-life accommodations has been well documented (Gappa, Austin, & Trice, 2007; Quinn, Lange, & Olswang, 2004). Such policies also must be institutionalized and a part of the university's culture (Mason & Goulden, 2004; Sullivan, Hollenshead, & Smith, 2004). If an organization's culture does not support work-life flexibility, employees may still feel pressure to conform to the ideal worker model, regardless of the existence of such policies (Thompson, 2008). Kossek, Lewis, & Hammer (2010) noted that structural and cultural work-life supports can force organizations to challenge the notion of the ideal worker and the emphasis on face time that pervades so many workplaces. Today's constant connectivity concerns must be given consideration in structural and cultural work-life supports.

As long as the commitment and productivity of employees is judged by time logged at the office or via a constant technological presence, an emphasis on face time in the physical or virtual office will persist. As Bailyn (1993) advocates, organizations need to value working smarter over working longer hours; however, our newfound ability to be constantly connected requires us to rethink exactly what working smarter means. Can and should we set parameters around the use of technology before and after traditional work hours? How can we devise work-life policies that give consideration to constant connectivity? How can we reframe ideal worker norms around working smarter instead of working constantly?

Perhaps at least part of the answer lies in previous research that shows the need to judge employees' performance by their results not by face time (Catalyst, 2001; Hochschild & Machung, 1989/2003). According to Harrington and Ladge (2009), corporate cultures continue to value time spent at work over individual efforts, which hampers the retention and promotion of women and other employees who demand greater flexibility over their schedules. This allows organizations to ignore the contributions of employees who may not put the organization before all needs but remain productive, valuable, reliable employees (Thompson, 2008). In this study, administrators with and without some degree of informal workplace flexibility desired to challenge ideal worker norms in their work areas and to replace existing norms with a work environment that emphasized results.

Limitations and Recommendations

The findings from this study cannot be generalized to administrators at other institutions or even to the broad population of administrators at Plains University. The design of this study could be tested, however, on administrators who work in other areas of Plains University and at other institutions. The findings from this study suggest that there are several steps that institutions, supervisors, and administrators can take to improve the work-life experience. Administrators, particularly those in Student Affairs, should engage in conversation with their supervisors regarding expectations for attendance at evening and weekend events. Administrators should also seek clarification from their supervisors surrounding expectations for technological responsiveness. Supervisors can take the lead on these conversations by clarifying face-time and technological expectations with their administrators, particularly through the facilitation of a conversation about these issues in large departmental or divisional meeting. Supervisors also must model the behavior that they wish their administrators to adopt regarding face-time and technological responsiveness.

At an institution with few work-life policies for administrators, like Plains University, supervisors can create an environment that emphasizes work results over physical or technological face time. These measures will help to challenge existing ideal worker norms, however, institutions also must play a role in conversations regarding work-life, face-time expectations, and technological responsiveness. Structural and cultural work-life policies and supports must be both implemented and adopted.

The ideal worker model that persists for faculty in the academy remains well entrenched for administrators who work in the Division of Technology and in the Division of Student Affairs at Plains University. As new generations of administrators with different values assume positions in the academy, the existence of work-life balance accommodations for administrators may become increasingly important. Greater recognition of and attention to administrators' work-life balance experiences and their perceptions of the ideal worker may better position the academy for the future and enable it to retain and to support a diverse administrative workforce.

References

Allen, T. (2008). Integrating career development and work-family policy. In S. A. Y. Poelmans, & P. Caligiuri (Eds.), *Harmonizing work, family, and personal life: From policy to practice* (pp. 19–38). Cambridge, England: Cambridge University Press.

Anderson, D. M., Morgan, B. L., & Wilson, J. B. (2002). Perceptions of family-friendly policies: University versus corporate employees. *Journal of Family and Economic Issues, 23*(1), 73–92.

Bailey, J. M. (2008). Work and life balance: Community college occupational deans. *Community College Journal of Research and Practice, 32*, 778–792.

Bailyn, L. (1993). *Breaking the mold: Women, men, and time in the new corporate world.* New York, NY: The Free Press.

Bailyn, L., Drago, R., & Kochan, T. (2001). *Integrating work and family life: A holistic approach.* Cambridge, MA: Massachusetts Institute of Technology, Sloan School of Management.

Barnett, R. C. (1998). Toward a review and reconceptualization of the work/family literature. *Genetic, Social, and General Psychology Monographs, 124*(2), 125–182.

Bess, J. L., & Dee, J. R. (2008). *Understanding college and university organization* (Vols. 1–2). Sterling, VA: Stylus Publishing.

Casper, W. J., Eby, L. T., Bordeaux, C., Lockwood, A., & Lambert, D. (2007). A review of research methods in IO/OB work-family research. *Journal of Applied Psychology, 92*(1), 28–43.

Catalyst. (2001). *The new generation: Today's professionals, tomorrow's leaders.* New York, NY: Catalyst.

Clark, S. C. (2000). Work/family border theory: A new theory of work/family balance. *Human Relations, 53*(6), 747–770.

Currie, J., & Eveline, J. (2011). E-technology and work/life balance for academics with young children. *Higher Education, 62*(4), 533–550.

Deal, J. J. (2013). *Always on, never done? Don't blame the smartphone.* Retrieved from Center for Creative Leadership website: http://www.ccl.org/leadership/pdf/research/AlwaysOn.pdf

Elsbach, K. D., Cable, D. M., & Sherman, J. W. (2010). How passive "face time" affects perceptions of employees: Evidence of spontaneous trait inference. *Human Relations, 63*(6), 735–760.

Finkel, S. K., & Olswang, S. G. (1996). Child rearing as a career impediment to women assistant professors. *The Review of Higher Education, 19*(2), 123–139.

Forney, D., Wallace-Schutzman, F., & Wiggers, T. T. (1982). Burnout among career development professionals: Preliminary findings and implications. *Personnel and Guidance Journal, 60*(7), 435–439.

Gappa, J. M., Austin, A. E., & Trice, A. G. (2007). *Rethinking faculty work: Higher education's strategic imperative.* San Francisco, CA: Jossey-Bass.

Gillespie, N. A., Walsh, M., Winefield, A. H., Dua, J., & Stough, C. (2001). Occupational stress in universities: Staff perceptions of the causes, consequences and moderators of stress. *Work and Stress, 15*(1), 53–72.

Grant, L., Kennelly, I., & Ward, K. B. (2000). Revisiting the gender, marriage, and parenthood puzzle in scientific careers. *Women's Studies Quarterly, 28*(1–2), 62–85.

Grotto, A. R. (2015). On-demand: When work intrudes upon employees' personal time—Does gender matter? In M. Mills (Ed.), *Gender and the work-family experience: An intersection of two domains* (pp. 201–223). New York, NY: Springer.

Harrington, B., & Ladge, J. J. (2009). Got talent? It isn't hard to find. *The Shriver report: A woman's nation changes everything*. Retrieved from: http://www.americanprogress.org/issues/2009/10/pdf/awn/a_womans_nation.pdf

Harrington, B., Van Deusen, F., & Ladge, J. (2010). *The new dad: Exploring fatherhood within a career context*. Retrieved from Boston College Center for Work & Family website: http://www.bc.edu/centers/cwf/meta-elements/pdf/BCCWF_Fatherhood_Study_The_New_Dad1.pdf

Herman, J. B., & Gyllstrom, K. K. (1977). Working men and women: Inter- and intra-role conflict. *Psychology of Women Quarterly, 1*(4), 319–333.

Hewlett, S. A. (2007). *Off-ramps and on-ramps: Keeping talented women on the road to success*. Boston, MA: Harvard Business School Press.

Hochschild, A. R., & Machung, A. (1989/2003). *The second shift* (2nd ed.). New York, NY: Penguin.

Jo, V. (2008). Voluntary turnover and women administrators in higher education. *Higher Education, 56*, 565–582.

Kossek, E. E. (in press). Managing work life boundaries in the digital age [Special issue]. *Organizational Dynamics*. Retrieved from: https://www.krannert.purdue.edu/directory/publications.asp?id=103032

Kossek, E. E., Lewis, S., & Hammer, L. B. (2010). Work-life initiatives and organizational change: Overcoming mixed messages to move from the margin to the mainstream. *Human Relations, 63*(1), 3–19.

LeCompte, M. D., & Goetz, J. P. (2007). Problems of reliability and validity in ethnographic research. In A. Bryman (Ed), *Qualitative research II* (Vol. I, pp. 3–39). San Francisco, CA: Jossey-Bass.

Lorden, L. (1998). Attrition in the student affairs profession. *NASPA Journal, 35*(3), 207–216.

Mason, M. A., & Goulden, M. (2004). Marriage and baby blues: Redefining gender equity in the academy. *The ANNALS of the American Academy of Political and Social Science, 596*, 86–103. doi:10.1177/0002716204268744

Matos, K., & Galinsky, E. (2011). *Workplace flexibility in the United States: A status report*. Retrieved from Families and Work Institute website: http://familiesandwork.org/site/research/reports/www_us_workflex.pdf

Quinn, K., Lange, S. E., & Olswang, S. G. (2004). Family-friendly policies and the research university. *Academe, 90*(6), 32–35.

Rappoport, R., Bailyn, L., Fletcher, J. K., & Pruitt, B. H. (2002). *Beyond work-family balance: Advancing gender equity and workplace performance*. San Francisco, CA: Jossey-Bass.

Rhoades, G. (2007). Making distinctive choices in intersecting markets: Seeking niches. In R. L. Geiger, C. L. Colbeck, R. L. Williams, & C. K. Anderson (Eds.), *Future of the American public research university* (pp. 121–143). Rotterdam, The Netherlands: Sense Publishers.

Rhoades, G., & Sporn, B. (2002). New models of management and shifting modes and costs of production: Europe and the United States. *Tertiary Education and Management, 8*(1), 3–28.

Rice, R. E., Sorcinelli, M. D., & Austin, A. E. (2000). *Heeding new voices: Academic careers for a new generation*. New Pathways Working Paper No. 7. Washington, DC: American Association for Higher Education.

Sallee, M. W. (2013). Gender norms and institutional culture: The family-friendly versus the father-friendly university. *The Journal of Higher Education, 84*(3), 363–396.

Sallee, M. W. (2012). The ideal worker or the ideal father: Organizational structures and culture in the gendered university. *Research in Higher Education, 53*(7), 782–802.

Sorcinelli, M. D., & Near, J. P. (1989). Relations between work and life away from work among university faculty. *The Journal of Higher Education, 60*(1), 59–81.

Sullivan, B., Hollenshead, C., & Smith, G. (2004). Developing and implementing work-family polices for faculty. *Academe, 90*(6). Retrieved from http://www.aaup.org/AAUP/pubres/academe/2004/ND/Feat/04ndsulli.htm

Thompson, C. A. (2008). Barriers to the implementation and usage of work-life policies. In S. A. Y. Poelmans, & P. Caligiuri (Eds.), *Harmonizing work, family, and personal life: From policy to practice* (pp. 19–38). Cambridge, England: Cambridge University Press.

Tracy, S. J. (2010). Qualitative quality: Eight "big tent" criteria for excellent qualitative research. *Qualitative Inquiry, 16*, 837–851. doi:10.1177/1077800410383121

Williams, J. (2000). *Unbending gender: Why family and work conflict and what to do about it.* New York, NY: Oxford University Press.

Winefield, A. H., Gillespie, N., Stough, C., Dua, J., Hapuarachchi, J., & Boyd, C. (2003). Occupational stress in Australian university staff: Results from a national survey. *International Journal of Stress Management, 10*(1), 51–63.

Winston, R. B., Jr., Creamer, D. G., & Miller, T. K. (2001). *The professional student affairs administrator: Educator, leader, and manager.* New York, NY: Brunner-Routledge.

KELLY E. WILK spent nearly a decade working in administrative positions in the academy. She currently consults for individuals and institutions.

This chapter explores the consequences of ideal worker norms for graduate student-parents in higher education and student affairs programs. Using Schein's (2004) levels of culture as a conceptual lens, this chapter considers the ways that programmatic structures and interactions with faculty and peers reflect and reproduce a culture across graduate programs that privileges the norm of the always-working and engaged student, thereby creating barriers to full participation for students with children.

Ideal for Whom? A Cultural Analysis of Ideal Worker Norms in Higher Education and Student Affairs Graduate Programs

Margaret W. Sallee

Master's students comprise nearly 65% of all graduate students in the United States (National Center for Education Statistics [NCES], 2010). However, with few exceptions (Conrad, Haworth, & Millar, 1993; Glazer-Raymo, 2005), higher-education scholarship has ignored their experiences. Master's students are a diverse group. One in three is a parent. Half are over the age of 30. Nine out of 10 work at least part-time, and two out of three are employed full-time (NCES, 2010). Many master's students fulfill a variety of roles that extend beyond that of student. Yet, graduate programs require significant commitment from students to complete course and degree requirements. In part, these expectations are informed by an assumption that graduate students have unlimited time to work with no other demands, such as jobs, spouses, or children. In other words, master's students are expected to be ideal workers.

Ideal worker norms are based on two assumptions: (1) the ideal employee is always available and working; and (2) the ideal employee is childless—or at least has a spouse at home to take care of family obligations (Hochschild, 1995). The main premises—expectations of a tireless, child-free worker—have implications for students who wish to balance family and work (or, in the case of students, academic obligations) (Acker, 1990; Hochschild, 1995; Williams, 2000). Many master's students contend with balancing multiple roles, including but not limited to student, parent,

New Directions for Higher Education, no. 176, Winter 2016 © 2016 Wiley Periodicals, Inc.
Published online in Wiley Online Library (wileyonlinelibrary.com) • DOI: 10.1002/he.20209

spouse, and employee. Rarely are students considered to be subject to ideal worker norms. It is the aim of this chapter to consider how they are affected by such norms.

I focus on master's students pursuing degrees in higher education and student affairs (HE/SA), a group that faces unique challenges combining academics and family. Several studies have noted the intense time demands placed on those working in student affairs (Marshall, 2009; Nobbe & Manning, 1997); often employment in these fields relies on employees working late at night and on weekends. The same hallmarks filter down to students in graduate programs. Master's programs in HE/SA are professional programs, designed to prepare students to work as administrators and educators on college and university campuses. As such, degree programs typically emphasize a combination of classroom learning and practical experience gained through assistantships and internships. Many HE/SA master's programs adhere to guidelines set forth by the Council for the Advancement of Standards, an accrediting body for the student affairs field, which recommend that a degree program consist of 40 to 48 credit hours plus 300 hours of supervised practical experience. With such demands, academic and work obligations often take precedence, leaving little time for personal obligations. These facts suggest that the ideal worker has a stronghold in HE/SA graduate programs as well.

However, students do not simply learn how to be ideal workers in a vacuum. Rather, they learn about the expectations of graduate work through interactions with faculty and peers who transmit the disciplinary values and norms (Weidman, Twale, & Stein, 2001); some of the norms include the compatibility of academics and parenting. In this chapter, I argue that the culture of graduate programs in HE/SA relies on the construct of students as ideal workers; programmatic structures along with interactions with faculty and peers reinforce these expectations. I begin by reviewing the role that faculty and peers play in the graduate student experience before turning to Schein's (2004) discussion of culture, which I use as an analytical lens. After discussing methodology, I turn to my findings, which illustrate how higher education and student affairs graduate programs reinforce ideal worker norms.

Key Actors in Graduate Education

Many factors shape students' experiences in graduate school: disciplinary culture, institutional culture, and a variety of actors, including faculty, peers, family, employers, and professional associations (Weidman, Twale, & Stein, 2001). In what follows, I outline the roles that faculty and peers play in the lives of student-parents pursuing graduate study in HE/SA.

New Directions for Higher Education • DOI: 10.1002/he

Faculty

Faculty play a critical role in preparing graduate students for their new roles (Austin, 2002; Bieber & Worley, 2006; Golde, 2000; Golde & Dore, 2001; Weidman & Stein, 2003). Student–faculty interactions take many forms, including interactions inside the classroom, casual conversations in hallways, and collaboration on research projects. Students learn simply through overhearing conversations or observing interactions between faculty and others in the department (Austin, 2002; Bieber & Worley, 2006). Students' interactions with faculty change as they progress through the program; beginning students have less frequent interactions with faculty than do more advanced students (Baird, 1992).

Faculty are pivotal in shaping the experiences of students with children (Brown & Nichols, 2013; Lynch, 2008; Robertson & Weiner, 2013; Wilson, 1997). Respondents to a survey of 414 student-parents reported that faculty were not accommodating if a family-related emergency arose that prevented students from attending class or turning in an assignment (Robertson & Weiner, 2013). Similarly, nearly all participants in another study wished that faculty were more understanding of the challenges of balancing doctoral study with motherhood (Lynch, 2008). Although some studies reported instances of faculty who were supportive—such as some in Wilson's (1997) study who changed the times that courses met to accommodate the demands of those with children—more frequently, research suggests that faculty are not understanding of the added difficulties faced by students with children.

Peers. Although faculty play a critical role in shaping the graduate experience, peers also transmit norms and attitudes (Austin, 2002; Baird, 1992; Golde, 2000; Weidman & Stein, 2003). Students look to their peers to make sense of their experiences in graduate school, interacting with their peers more than with faculty. In Weidman and Stein's (2003) survey of 50 doctoral students in two disciplines, 84% of respondents reported engaging in social conversation with faculty versus 91% who had social conversations with peers. Additionally, whereas 69% of respondents reported discussions in their field or other topics of intellectual interest with a faculty member, 85% reported having such conversations with their peers. Clearly, peers play a significant role in shaping students' experiences in their graduate programs.

However, the literature suggests that students with children do not always feel supported by their peers and instead may feel isolated from them (Lynch, 2008; Robertson & Weiner, 2013; Wilson, 1997). For example, Lynch (2008) found that students who were the sole student-parents in their department reported feeling isolated and dissatisfied with peer relationships. In a study of student-parents at a community college, Wilson and Cox (2011) found that students taking courses with traditional-age students felt isolated, whereas those who took courses with other student-parents experienced more support.

As the literature illustrates, although faculty help students learn the skills necessary for success in graduate school, students interact more frequently with their peers. However, such interactions are not always positive for students with children, thereby creating an unwelcoming culture.

Studying Culture

Culture shapes the way that organizational life unfolds. Many have studied culture and its impact on organizations, broadly, and higher-education institutions, in particular (Kezar, 2001). For this cultural analysis, I rely upon Schein's (2004) approach to culture, which suggests that culture operates at three levels: artifacts, values, and assumptions. Artifacts are the observable aspects of culture while values and assumptions are invisible, but can be intuited from an analysis of artifacts.

Artifacts.   The culture of an organization is reflected in all visible parts of an organization, ranging from the conditions of the buildings to the ways that people interact with each other. Schein (2004) identified six types of artifacts: (1) physical environment, (2) social environment, (3) technology, (4) written and spoken language, (5) behavior of group members, and (6) symbols.

Social environment focuses on the nature of relationships between members of an organization, such as whether relationships are collegial or strained. Relationships between particular groups—such as faculty and students—reflect the culture of a department. A department in which faculty treat graduate students as adults with outside lives has a different culture than a department that focuses solely on students' academic responsibilities.

Technology focuses on the ways in which inputs are transformed into outputs. In academic departments, technology includes the ways that entering students are transformed into graduates. Most graduate programs focus on small seminars that require student participation rather than large lectures characterized by the passive receipt of information. Graduate programs in HE/SA frequently privilege practical experience as a necessary component of the degree program, which leads to marketable skills, but also places additional stress on students.

Written and spoken language includes the ways that organizational members speak to and address one another, such as whether faculty are addressed by their first names or their titles. Language also includes the stories that are told among groups. For example, if students who work long hours are praised over those who limit their work hours, this sends a particular message about the values of the discipline.

Behavior of group members focuses on the types of behaviors that are valued and rewarded by an organization. In the earlier example, if a department frequently praises students who work long hours, other students may adopt similar behaviors in an attempt to receive similar rewards.

Finally, colleges and universities are rife with *symbols*, including campus mascots and statues of organizational heroes. A campus with statues of only White men sends different messages than a campus with statues of men and women of multiple races. Taken together, artifacts help reveal the values and assumptions of an organization.

Values and Assumptions.   Values can be inferred from analysis of cultural artifacts, whereas assumptions are unconscious and embedded in organizational structures (Schein, 2004). Assumptions can be deduced from an analysis of values. Returning to the earlier example of praising students who work long hours, such stories and behaviors suggest a department that values students who prioritize work over other obligations. Such values also point to assumptions of the ideal worker; students are expected to have no other demands on their time. A department offering courses that regularly require students to engage in group work outside of class signals a focus on collaborative values. Such values might point to assumptions about the importance of building relationships and a belief that learning takes place through multiple forms.

Engaging in a cultural analysis requires reviewing multiple artifacts to understand how they point to particular values and assumptions. In this analysis, I use Schein's (2004) artifacts of technology, the social environment, and overt behaviors of faculty and peers to understand the extent to which ideal worker norms are implicit in the culture of graduate education in HE/SA and the implications of these norms for students with children.

Methodology

I approached this qualitative case study from an interpretive perspective informed by Merriam's (1998) definition of case study. Case studies are defined by a "bounded system" in which the object of inquiry has clear boundaries. Furthermore, interpretive case studies use descriptive data to "illustrate, support, or challenge theoretical assumptions" (p. 197). In this study, I define HE/SA programs as the case. Although each program has its own culture, all prepare practitioners to enter the field of HE/SA and thus have a shared disciplinary culture. Given that I use the concept of the ideal worker to understand the experiences of student-parents, this study meets Merriam's (1998) criteria for an interpretive case study.

Participant Recruitment.   Participants were required to (a) be enrolled in HE/SA master's programs, (b) have at least one child under the age of 18, and (c) be employed in an assistantship or have a full-time job on a campus. Participants were sought through emails to higher-education faculty, seeking their aid in identifying student-parents, along with announcements to multiple listservs, including ACPA's Standing

Committee for Graduate Students and New Professionals and NASPA's New Professionals and Graduate Students Knowledge Community.

A total of 18 participants—12 women and 6 men—from 10 universities around the United States completed interviews. Participants ranged in age from 24 to 52, though the majority were in their late 20s and early 30s. Participants had between one and four children, ranging in age from infancy to 18; 11 participants had one child, six had two, and one had four children. All but one of the participants were married. Ten participants were enrolled full-time while eight were part-time students. Fourteen participants worked full-time and four held graduate assistantships.

Methods.   Interviews constituted the primary method of data collection. Interviews typically lasted between 45 minutes and an hour; nearly all occurred over the phone, were recorded, and later transcribed. Questions probed participants' experiences balancing academic study, work, and family along with their perceptions about their program's support for student-parents. A review of program websites provided further data for analysis, allowing me to gain a greater understanding of the expectations associated with each program and the potential challenges that students might face.

Data Analysis.   Data analysis was both concept-driven, using predetermined codes generated from the literature, and data-driven, generating codes from the data (Kvale & Brinkmann, 2009). Examples of concept-driven codes included "faculty supportive" and "faculty unsupportive." Examples of data-driven codes included "connections with other nontraditional students" and "after-hours socials." I used atlas.ti, a qualitative data analysis software, to code the data and organize the codes into various families, such as "agents" and "programmatic/structural supports and barriers." The codes from both of these families inform this chapter.

Trustworthiness.   Enhanced credibility of findings' trustworthiness was sought through triangulation and member checks (Lincoln & Guba, 1985). I engaged in triangulation by checking the claims that participants made about their programs with information available on websites. I also shared findings with participants and sought their feedback.

Limitations.   A few limitations arise from this study. First, the experiences of these 18 participants did not capture all potential participants; those who were excluded or opted not to participate may differ from those who did. My decision not to interview faculty in the various programs may strike some as a limitation. However, given that I was interested in focusing on student perceptions and that I used institutional websites to corroborate students' claims, I maintain that the data faithfully represent the experiences of participants.

Some might take exception to my treatment of multiple HE/SA programs as one case. Individual campus culture differences are ignored in favor of examining the broader culture of HE/SA programs. As participants' experiences confirm, student-parents across study sites expressed the same concerns about the ways that the culture of their graduate programs expected students to devote themselves to their studies, often at the expense of their families.

Findings

Participants noted many challenges in combining parenthood and academics. At times, they praised faculty for providing instrumental support, though some still felt marginalized by their program's community. Nowhere was this exclusion more evident than in their relationship with their peers. I discuss how interactions with faculty and peers along with programmatic features point to a culture in which the student role is given primacy over other life roles.

Faculty and Programmatic Interactions.   Participants listed many ways that their faculty and courses both facilitated and hindered their success in their programs. The majority of participants reported being happy with both the emotional and instrumental support provided by professors related to students' roles as parents. However, some participants were less enthusiastic about the times that courses were offered and some of their professors' pedagogical choices—namely, group projects.

Although many participants noted that their professors were supportive of student-parents, some students noted an absence of support, such as one mother who stated, "I know all of my professors know that I'm a parent and that I have a child and [that fact has] not been communicated to me in any fashion. So I think that that's not okay." Although five participants noted instances of negative or neutral interactions about family issues with faculty, 13 noted ways in which they, or other classmates with children, had been supported by faculty. Students described both instrumental acts of support, such as changing an assignment due date, as well as support that came through simply being able to talk through their concerns about balancing school and family. One mother was effusive about the support of her professors:

> Because the faculty are parents too ... they understand how crazy the schedule is and what it's like to have a newborn. ... The director of our program, he has two kids. And this one professor that I have right now, he has two kids. And so, when we'll run into each other in the parking lot ... they can relate to the crazy schedule and how exciting it is.

This mother commented throughout the interview how much she appreciated that her professors acknowledged the demands of raising children, but provided support in other ways, such as granting an incomplete on an assignment when she gave birth early. She was not the only one to note the support of faculty in such instrumental acts.

Eight students reported acts of support in flexibility with due dates and absences caused by parenting issues. One student discovered that she was pregnant shortly after being admitted to the program and was due to give birth at the end of December. As both she and one of her classmates described in separate interviews, faculty made arrangements for her to finish her coursework and take final exams before Thanksgiving to accommodate her due date. Other participants noted with gratitude when faculty gave them short extensions that enabled them to get their work done.

There were occasions when child-care mix-ups interfered with class time. Occasionally, students brought their children to class, as this father explained. "I've also had [other] parents in my program that have needed to bring their kids to class. ... Nobody's ever given, you know, any indication other than that they were being supportive." Although such events were unusual, participants across programs reported that they frequently felt supported by faculty in navigating both their parental and academic demands and in-class activities.

Although students were generally satisfied with the support they received from faculty, many were less satisfied with features of their programs and coursework. Two thirds of participants were in graduate programs that were designed to appeal to the working adult; nearly all courses were offered in the late afternoon and evening hours. Many of the participants noted that such a schedule was problematic for students with children, particularly those who could not rely on family for child care. One mother recounted the challenges that one of her friends, a single mother, faced in selecting courses:

> My friend who is a single mom ... she can never take that class because she doesn't have child care from 4 to 7. ... Luckily, I have a husband who can do that. But if I didn't? What would I have done? Would I have had to hire a babysitter every single ... week for that class? That would be impossible.

Participants noted that although evening class times appealed to the working adult, they were not designed with the needs of those with child-care responsibilities in mind. Rather, students were assumed to be childless or to have someone else available to care for children, like the ideal worker. Additionally, none of the programs explicitly communicated ways students might navigate possible conflicts between course times and parenting duties.

Although course times proved problematic for some, nearly half of participants noted challenges that came with a major feature of many of their courses: group work. Participants explained that their multiple life demands made it difficult to fulfill outside meetings that were required of group projects. One mother described her work on a group presentation. "It's just one more pain to try to be away from the house on a weeknight. ... It puts strain in other areas—on my husband, on the kids, getting them from school and to him." Other parents reported missing time with their kids due to group work, like this father, who said, "I kind of have a disdain for [group work] right now because it's so hard for me with balancing my kids and the rest of my life to have to go meet people for group projects." As this father told me in another part of the interview, he understood the purpose of group projects, but found that they typically required extra demands on student-parents' already precious time. Although faculty were noted for providing emotional support to students and making small accommodations if students needed help, the standard structures and expectations of graduate coursework remained intact, creating barriers for students with children.

Peers.   Although participants reported mixed feelings about interactions with faculty and programmatic features, they were less positive about interactions with their classmates. Although some participants formed connections with other students in their program, the majority suggested that the differences in age, parental status, and part-time versus full-time status led them to feel disconnected from the majority of students in the program. Participants were most likely to form bonds with other nontraditional students, frequently other parents. They were typically unable to participate in social activities planned by their peers, though many wished that they had time to do so. The peer culture of the graduate programs focused on the childless graduate student, creating an unwelcoming space for those with familial obligations.

Although a handful of students described building connections with their traditional-age classmates, the majority of participants reported feeling separated from their classmates. Some participants were pursuing their degree on a part-time basis, which contributed to a sense of separation. One student explained:

> I'm a full-time employee, part-time student. I'm older. I'm not the typical student in our program that's coming in straight out of undergrad that gets a GA position on campus and is really involved in the graduate student association and all the activities.

She was not the only student to point to part-time status as contributing to a sense of separation. Another shared:

> Basically there is little to no interaction [with my classmates] .... Well, for one, because it's taken me longer and I was working on a slower pace than everyone else in my original cohort, they're all gone already. So, you know, the classes I'm in now, I don't even really know the students because I didn't start with them.

Given that nearly half the participants were pursuing their degrees on a part-time basis, many found themselves in classes with different groups of students, thus making it hard to form connections with their peers.

Many students also attributed the separation they felt to their age and parental status; both meant that they had acquired different life experiences than their younger peers. One participant explained how she had an easier time connecting with older students. "There are younger students in my cohort group, and I think sometimes it's harder to explain something to them. There are some that have children of their own and it's easy for me to connect with them right away." One father shared how he felt separated from his peers due to his age and previous experience in the military:

> At 24 years old, I was a sergeant. I had been busted already [demoted] once in rank. I was leading troops. I was a military medic. I'm now 45. There's a life experience for me folks that I've got to look at you and say "you guys have no idea how much you have in front of you."

Some student-parents felt that younger students did not bring maturity to their coursework, whereas others remarked that they had different life demands as a result of being older and raising children. Either way, they felt marked as different from their peers.

Many participants also noted that they were excluded from social interactions with their classmates, both inside and outside the classroom, as this father did:

> It was hard entering into [the classroom] last fall ... they all knew each other and they were all talking about stuff that I had never heard of before and continued to do that. It was like high school or middle school all over again.

This father felt excluded from his classmates' social interactions; he later shared that the only students with whom he connected were international students, who were similarly excluded from his classmates' conversations.

In addition to feeling excluded inside the classroom, many were unable to participate in formal and informal out-of-class activities with their classmates. Some parents, like this father, wanted to participate in the graduate student association affiliated with their programs, but could not due to family responsibilities:

> I want to be really involved in the extracurricular part of my graduate program, like [our] Graduate Student Association.... They'll get together once a week at a bar and grill and they'll do mixers and hang out. And they'll have stuff like writing sessions and brown bag seminars, and I can't go to any of that stuff because all of the free time that I would be going to that, I'm engaged with my kids and my wife.

This father was not the only one to note that he was not able to participate in activities outside the classroom. Another man noted that he was a "big proponent" of the outside activities his classmates planned, noting, "I'd really love to [attend,] but I can't afford the energy, let alone the time."

Participants felt most able to connect with other student-parents. In most programs, parents represented just a handful of students, though in one program, one father said that of the 20 students in his program, seven had kids. Such large numbers were more the exception than the norm. In each case, participants turned to other student-parents for emotional and academic support. As one mother said, "There are some that have children of their own, and it's easy for me to connect with them right away or immediately." Another mother said, "There are a few people that are in my program right now as well that are also parents. ... We kind of have a network, you know?" Another mother explained how a small group of parents had "formed [their] own little cohort" and supported each other with academic and family demands. Although their younger classmates shared experiences around late-night study sessions or happy hours at bars, the student-parents shared experiences around their identities and responsibilities to their children.

In sum, students with children had mixed experiences in their graduate programs. They appreciated the support they received from faculty but felt marginalized by their classmates and unable to participate in most out-of-class activities. Additionally, some of the structures of the program, including course times and pedagogies favored by their professors, proved less than welcoming for students with children.

Discussion

Past research has suggested that student-parents face challenges in navigating academic study. Many have noted that student-parents often feel isolated from other students in their programs (Lynch, 2008; Robertson & Weiner, 2013; Wilson, 1997). Participants in this study were no different. The majority of participants suggested that they felt separated from their traditional-age peers. Unlike previous research reporting that faculty were not understanding of students who had to miss class or turn in an assignment late due to child-related issues (Robertson & Weiner, 2013), participants in this study praised their faculty for their support, particularly around academic matters.

However, findings also suggest that the culture of graduate programs in HE/SA is not entirely welcoming to students with children. Many students felt excluded by their peers and challenged by the built-in requirements of their programs. Although they enjoyed their programs, many felt as if they did not belong. In part, graduate students with children experienced a mismatch as graduate study expects students to be ideal workers, or always working and with no family responsibilities (Acker, 1990; Williams, 2000). Using Schein's (2004) levels of culture, I examine the ways in which artifacts of these programs underscore deep-seated assumptions of the ideal worker.

Although individual faculty may have tried to support graduate students with children, few elements of the program suggested that the culture was welcoming for those who differ from the norm. Such lack of support was evident in the artifact of **technology**, or the way that inputs are transformed into outputs. Although courses in the majority of the programs were offered in the late afternoons and evenings to appeal to working adults, this time slot was not as useful for students with children. As participants commented, child-care centers are not open in the evenings, thus leaving students to rely on family members to care for children. However, for students without such support or money to pay for care, such obstacles may be prohibitive to enrollment or completion.

Group work, another example of **technology**, also proved problematic for many participants. Although a favored pedagogical tool of professors, student-parents lamented that such projects added more time demands to already packed schedules. Multiple group projects signal that a program **values** teamwork and collaboration. However, they also signal an expectation that students are able to put course demands above all other responsibilities, underscoring the degree to which graduate programs reinforce ideal worker norms.

Social environment and *overt behaviors* were both evident in the ways in which participants interacted with their professors and their peers. Students generally noted that their interactions with faculty were positive. Some appreciated simply being able to talk about parenting with their professors. Others recounted that faculty had changed due dates to accommodate parenting demands. Occasionally, students brought their kids with them into class. All these acts are notable and important. However, these acts are not enough to change the culture into one that values parenting.

Participants generally felt excluded from out-of-class interactions. Many students noted that they could not participate in professional development opportunities. In some cases, professional development was offered at inconvenient times and in others, they simply could not afford the time away from their children. In all cases, students missed out. Nowhere did students feel more excluded than in interactions with their peers. The majority of participants suggested that their program was designed for their younger and childless peers. One student recalled the cliques he witnessed in the classroom. Others recounted the numerous social events that were held at times (nights) and locations (bars) that made attending with children impossible. To counterbalance this exclusion, some students formed connections with other student-parents. However, these groups were small and did not constitute enough of a critical mass to change the culture of the programs.

The experiences of participants suggest that the culture of graduate programs in HE/SA is unwelcoming to students with children. Instead, the structure of the programs and the people within them reinforce the *assumption* that the most successful student is one who embodies the traits of the ideal worker. Evening courses without available child care, group projects that require students to meet out of class, and professional development opportunities that take place at inconvenient times also are based on the assumption that students have countless hours to give to coursework. For their part, the traditional-age graduate students reinforced this message, particularly through their social functions outside of the classroom that excluded their parenting peers. Although faculty made efforts to support participants, the overall culture remained intact as one that expects a lot of all students, including those who already have significant life roles off campus.

Implications and Conclusion

Although participants reported benefiting from some elements of support, particularly from faculty, findings suggest ways in which HE/SA programs might be even more supportive of student-parents. First, programs might consider creating minicohorts of nontraditional students, including students with children. Given that many participants suggested they felt isolated from their traditional-age peers and were only one of a handful of students with children in their programs, students might benefit from taking courses with other students like them. Such repeated contact would allow students to develop relationships that may better integrate them into the programmatic community and contribute to a sense of belonging. Although students felt supported by faculty, many felt that excessive group work was a burden on their personal lives. Faculty who are committed to group work as a pedagogical tool might consider allotting additional time for group work during class or encourage students to find alternative ways to fulfill the aims of the assignment, such as holding group meetings via Skype, Google Hangouts, or other online platforms.

Creating family-friendly events for students with children serves as another way to integrate all students into the program's community. Not only would such events allow parents to connect with other parents, but it would also allow parents to interact with their traditional-age peers in a social setting. Potential events might include having a picnic at a park or other child-friendly venues. By sponsoring events at times that are convenient for many students and in a family-friendly locale, programs transmit the message that all parts of students' lives—the academic and the personal—are valued parts of their identities and, therefore, valued parts of the program community.

Findings from this study suggest avenues for further research. Future studies might include in-depth case studies of a purposefully selected sample of master's programs in HE/SA to understand how unique aspects of programmatic culture contribute to the student experience. Other studies might examine the experiences of master's students across disciplines, perhaps contrasting students in professional disciplines with those in science, math, and engineering fields. It is clear that the field is ripe for additional research. Regardless of the direction, however, it is time to acknowledge the pervasiveness of the construct of the ideal worker. No longer does it solely apply to those in paid employment, but it also is evident in expectations associated with graduate study. Although commitment to work and academic study is important, so is commitment to family and life outside the classroom. Given contemporary commitments to equity, it is time for programs to alter their structures and practices so that all students are valued members of the community and are encouraged to lead healthy and well-rounded lives.

References

Acker, J. (1990). Hierarchies, jobs, bodies: A theory of gendered organizations. *Gender and Society, 4*(2), 139–158.

Austin, A. E. (2002). Preparing the next generation of faculty: Graduate school as socialization to the academic career. *The Journal of Higher Education, 73*(1), 94–122.

Baird, L. L. (1992). *The stages of the doctoral career: Socialization and its consequences.* Paper presented at the Annual Meeting of the American Educational Research Association, San Francisco, CA: Jossey-Bass.

Bieber, J. P., & Worley, L. K. (2006). Conceptualizing the academic life: Graduate students' perspectives. *The Journal of Higher Education, 77*(6), 1009–1035.

Brown, V., & Nichols, T. R. (2013). Pregnant and parenting students on campus: Policy and program implications for a growing population. *Educational Policy, 27*(3), 499–530.

Conrad, C. F., Haworth, J. G., & Millar, S. M. (1993). *A silent success: Master's education in the United States.* Baltimore, MD: Johns Hopkins University Press.

Glazer-Raymo, J. (2005). *Professionalizing graduate education: The master's degree in the marketplace.* San Francisco, CA: Jossey-Bass.

Golde, C. M. (2000). Should I stay or should I go? Student descriptions of the doctoral attrition process. *The Review of Higher Education, 23*(2), 199–227.

Golde, C. M., & Dore, T. M. (2001). *At cross purposes: What the experiences of today's doctoral students reveal about doctoral education* (www.phd-survey.org). Philadelphia, PA: A report prepared by The Pew Charitable Trusts.

Hochschild, A. R. (1995). The culture of politics: Traditional, postmodern, cold-modern, and warm-modern ideals of care. *Social Politics, 2*, 331–346.

Kezar, A. J. (2001). *Understanding and facilitating organizational change in the 21st century: Recent research and conceptualizations.* San Francisco, CA: Jossey-Bass.

Kvale, S., & Brinkmann, S. (2009). *InterViews: Learning the craft of qualitative research interviewing* (2nd ed.). Thousand Oaks, CA: Sage.

Lincoln, Y. S., & Guba, E. G. (1985). *Naturalistic inquiry.* Newbury Park, CA: Sage.

Lynch, K. D. (2008). Gender roles and the American academe: A case study of graduate student mothers. *Gender and Education, 20*(6), 585–605.

Marshall, S. M. (2009). Women higher education administrators with children: Negotiating personal and professional lives. *NASPA Journal About Women in Higher Education, 2*(1), 188–221.

Merriam, S. B. (1998). *Qualitative research and case study applications in education.* San Francisco, CA: Jossey-Bass.

National Center for Education Statistics. (2010). *Profile of graduate and first-professional students: Trends from selected years, 1995–96 to 2007–08 (NCES 2011–219).* Washington, DC: Author.

Nobbe, J., & Manning, S. K. (1997). Issues for women in student affairs with children. *NASPA Journal*, *34*, 101–111.

Robertson, A. S., & Weiner, A. (2013). Building community for student-parents and their families: A social justice challenge for higher education. *Journal of Academic Perspectives*, *2013*(2), 1–21.

Schein, E. (2004). *Organizational culture and leadership* (3rd ed.). San Francisco, CA: Jossey-Bass.

Weidman, J. C., & Stein, E. L. (2003). Socialization of doctoral students to academic norms. *Research in Higher Education*, *44*(6), 641–656.

Weidman, J. C., Twale, D. J., & Stein, E. J. (2001). Socialization of graduate and professional students in higher education: A perilous passage? *ASHE-ERIC Higher Education Report*, *28*(3), San Francisco, CA: Jossey-Bass.

Williams, J. (2000). *Unbending gender: Why family and work conflict and what to do about it*. New York, NY: Oxford University Press.

Wilson, F. (1997). The construction of paradox?: One case of mature students in higher education. *Higher Education Quarterly*, *51*(4), 347–366.

Wilson, K. B., & Cox, E. M. (2011). No kids allowed: Transforming community colleges to support mothering. *NASPA Journal About Women in Higher Education*, *4*(2), 218–241.

MARGARET W. SALLEE *is associate professor of higher education at the University at Buffalo.*

5

Using Astin's (1993) College Impact Model, this chapter explores the current literature as it relates to single mothers in undergraduate postsecondary education. The chapter looks at the ways that undergraduates who are single mothers are counter to the "ideal-student" norms. Policy and best-practice recommendations conclude the chapter.

Undergraduate Single Mothers' Experiences in Postsecondary Education

Sydney Beeler

When asked to picture the prototypical undergraduate, the media, the public, and many researchers often describe the ideal student—one who is traditional aged, who attends full time, who lives on campus, who is involved in multiple on-campus activities, and who is dedicated solely to being a student. This "typical" student is the subject of most research literature, especially research focused on college student development, college success, and the college experience. The problem is that this literature fails to capture the majority of today's students who are not representative of that ideal. Today's students are older, attend part-time, work substantial hours, live off campus, and are otherwise defined as nontraditional. Indeed, nontraditional students now outnumber traditional students (National Center for Education Statistics [NCES], 2016), and yet researchers often neglect to use them in their samples. Because theories and research on college students often drive federal, state, and institutional policies and practices, failure to attend to the unique needs of nontraditional students is inherently problematic. This chapter focuses on a subset of nontraditional undergraduates—single mothers.

In the United States, there are approximately 3.4 million undergraduate student mothers, and almost 60% of them are single mothers (Gault, Reichlin, Reynolds, & Froehner, 2014). Single mothers are attending college at higher rates than ever before, but they face many obstacles in college success and completion (Huelsman & Engle, 2013; Nelson, Froehner, & Gault, 2013). Nelson, et al. (2013) report that 53% of student parents leave college within 6 years without a degree compared to 31% of their nonparent counterparts. Low-income student parents face additional challenges and

NEW DIRECTIONS FOR HIGHER EDUCATION, no. 176, Winter 2016   © 2016 Wiley Periodicals, Inc.
Published online in Wiley Online Library (wileyonlinelibrary.com) • DOI: 10.1002/he.20210

are 25% less likely to obtain their degrees compared to their low-income nonparent counterparts. Seventy-eight percent of single mothers are low-income, thus the risk factors and barriers they experience in postsecondary access and completion are significant. Although this population of students is increasing, their success and completion rates are not. It is important for college administrators, faculty, staff, and other students to gain a deeper understanding of single mothers' experiences and how institutions, through policy and programming, help or inhibit their success.

The purpose of this chapter is to better understand single mothers' experiences in undergraduate education. Utilizing Astin's (1993) college impact model, the chapter frames the literature on single mothers' experiences with an emphasis on assessing student growth or change. Astin (1993) asserts that student growth or change is "determined by comparing outcome characteristics with input characteristics" (p. 7), and the environment influences how student change or grow. This chapter reviews existing literature that seeks to answer the following questions:

1. What are the background characteristics of single mothers who are undergraduates? How are they similar to other student populations? How are they unique? How do their background characteristics influence their postsecondary experiences?
2. How do environmental conditions influence or inhibit successful access and completion of postsecondary education for single mothers?
3. What are the postsecondary outcomes for single mothers?

Background Characteristics of Undergraduate Single Mothers

Astin (1993) defined input characteristics as the "raw materials" one possesses prior to postsecondary education. Single mothers are distinctly different from their childless or dependent peers in terms of background characteristics, which can directly influence their ability to access and complete postsecondary education in comparable numbers and rates to their peers (e.g., Austin & McDermott, 2003; Cerven, 2013; Gault, Reichlin, & Roman, 2014; Huelsman & Engle, 2013; Radey & Cheatham, 2013; Zhan & Pandey, 2004a; 2004b). Single mothers are financially independent, are older than the age of 24, and are more likely to lack a high school diploma (NCES, 2002). If they attend college at all, they are likely to attend part-time. Huelsman and Engle (2013) report that single student parents, who are disproportionately single mothers (73.5%), have difficulties maintaining their enrollment for consecutive terms, thus delaying degree completion, if ever completing. Single mothers are more likely than their married or dependent counterparts to work and care for dependent children full-time (Huelsman & Engle, 2013). Part-time, interrupted attendance and the pressures of juggling work, school, and family responsibilities put single mothers at a disadvantage in accessing and completing postsecondary education compared to their nonparenting peers (NCES, 2002; Goldrick-Rab & Sorensen, 2010).

Single mothers who lack high school diplomas are also at a higher risk of failing to access or complete a degree. In Costello's (2014) review of pregnant and parenting teens, high school completion was the first challenge to postsecondary access. Costello found that only about half of teen mothers received their high school diploma by the age of 22. Data also indicate that pregnant and parenting teens are often academically unprepared. Goldrick-Rab & Sorensen (2010) note that 18% of single mothers, as compared to 6% of the overall population, begin college with a GED. Single mothers are also more likely than their nonparent and/or married counterparts to begin their education at a community college and require some developmental coursework (Costello, 2014; Gault et al., 2014; Goldrick-Rab & Sorensen, 2010; Huelsman & Engle, 2013).

Single mothers are more likely to be first generation and low income than their married counterparts with children and students who do not have children, and they share similar disadvantages: lack of knowledge about the college enrollment process, lack of knowledge about financial aid, the need to work, and lack of academic preparation (Costello, 2014; Goldrick-Rab & Sorensen, 2010; Huelsman & Engle, 2013). Like many low-income and first-generation college students, single mothers disproportionately come from racial and ethnically underrepresented backgrounds (Goldrick-Rab & Sorensen, 2010; Huelsman & Engle, 2013). Gault, Reichlin, Reynolds, et al. (2014) assert that, "[w]omen of color in postsecondary education are more likely than other college students to have dependent children; 47% of African American women students, 39.4% of Native American students, and 31.6% of Latina students are mothers" (p. 4).

Single mothers' background characteristics can influence their college experiences because they have often competing priorities as caretakers and employees along with being students (Austin & McDermott, 2003; Costello, 2014; Goldrick-Rab & Sorensen, 2010). Because higher-education settings prioritize, privilege, and reward students' dedication to their academic studies, mothers may face simultaneous, competing demands to be both ideal students and ideal parents. Being an "ideal student" is related to the concept of the ideal worker norm, which posits that ideal workers focus on work in lieu of other responsibilities (e.g., Hochschild, 1989). From an undergraduate perspective, the ideal student is traditional aged, attends full time, is not financially independent, and is free of outside responsibilities to focus on schoolwork (Wolf-Wendel & Ruel, 1999). Living up to the norm of the ideal student is difficult for single mothers with care-taking responsibilities; their time and focus must be divided between school, family, and often, work.

Although they are expected to be ideal students, single mothers are also expected to be "ideal parents." The concept of the ideal parent is influenced by normative cultural and social expectations regarding good parenting, whereby good parents must be highly attentive to their children, self-sacrificial of their own needs for their children's needs, and must provide stable financial, emotional, and developmental support for their children (Estes, 2011). In trying to live up to being both ideal students and ideal parents, single mothers may experience feelings of role conflict, guilt for time spent away from children, increased psychological distress including feeling overwhelmed or isolated, and financial stress (Austin & McDermott, 2003; Costello, 2014).

In the midst of pressure to maintain roles as ideal parents and ideal students, single mothers may be more likely to enroll in postsecondary education because they want to be positive role models and achieve stable financial support for their children. In this way, having a child may act as a motivator for them to access and complete degrees (Cerven, 2013; Costello, 2014; Duquaine-Watson, 2007; Osborne, Marks, & Turner, 2004; Wilsey, 2013; Wilson, 2011). For example, Osborne et al. (2004) interviewed single parents in the United Kingdom regarding their choices to enter or re-enter higher education. The primary motivator for single parents, especially single mothers, was the desire to be a good role model and provide an economically stable future for their children. These findings are consistent with studies on American single mothers (Cerven, 2013; Wilsey, 2013). These motivations and others influence single mothers to pursue postsecondary degrees despite their largely disadvantaged backgrounds, and once in a college or university, their experiences are mediated by a number of environmental influences that can assist or inhibit their success.

Environmental Influences

According to Astin (1993), "environment" encompasses all postsecondary factors that could affect the student. These factors include policies and procedures, curriculum and pedagogical practices, interactions with faculty, staff, and peers, and the overall climate. The environment can positively or negatively influence a student's success; however, a student's success can also be influenced by a combination of their background characteristics and the environment (Astin, 1993). The environment that single mothers experience is influenced by factors within the postsecondary institution's environment and by factors in the external environment (i.e., local, state, and federal policies, and supportive others; Cerven, 2013; Duquaine-Watson, 2007; Johnson, 2010; Schumacher, 2015).

Policy.   Many single mothers use postsecondary education as a way out of poverty (Goldrick-Rab & Sorensen, 2010; Lovell, 2014; Pandey, Zahn, & Kim, 2006; Radey & Cheatham, 2013; Romo & Segura, 2010; Zhan & Pandey, 2004a; 2004b). Falling below the poverty level makes single mothers vulnerable to changes in federal, state, and institutional policies, specifically welfare and financial aid policies (Duquaine-Watson, 2007; Cerven, 2013; Costello, 2014; Fenster, 2003; Huelsman & Engle, 2013;

Johnson, 2010). The Personal Responsibility and Work Opportunity Reconciliation Act (PRWORA) promoted a work-first policy, thereby making it a challenge for some single mothers to attend college (Duquaine-Watson, 2007; Johnson, 2010). Although welfare reform decreased the number of welfare recipients enrolling in postsecondary education (Duquaine-Watson, 2007; Johnson, 2010), the enrollment rates of single mothers increased, especially at community colleges (Gault et al., 2014; Huelsman & Engle, 2013; Wilson, 2011). Such incongruences caused Wilson (2011) to investigate how 10 low-income single mothers used benefits from 20 different educational and noneducational programs. The interviewees needed to work while being enrolled in postsecondary education and relied on resources from social benefit programs such as food stamps. Federal financial aid programs, such as the Pell Grant, were especially important for single mothers in their individual college decision-making processes because the utilization of Temporary Assistance for Needy Families (TANF) inhibited them in the college choice process. Finally, the lack of clear and correct information regarding the benefits, eligibility requirements, and application procedures for both educational and noneducational benefit programs led Wilson (2011) to conclude that it is a lack of clarity, collaboration, communication, and knowledge among federal, state, and local agencies and postsecondary institutions that inhibits single mothers' access. Like many federal and state policies, changes in welfare laws are often poorly communicated and misunderstood.

Financial aid plays a pivotal role in postsecondary access and completion for undergraduate single mothers (Cerven, 2013; Huelsman & Engle, 2013; Radey & Cheatham, 2013; Wilson, 2011). Single mothers are at an increased risk for not completing the Free Application for Federal Student Aid (FAFSA), which inhibits their access to needed assistance (Huelsman & Engle, 2013; Radey & Cheatham, 2013). Radey and Cheatham (2013) explored how student background characteristics—marital status, number of children, level of income, and employment—influenced FAFSA completion for 27,269 students. They found that when all vulnerabilities were accounted for, single mothers had the lowest rates of FAFSA completion. Radey and Cheatham's (2013) study supports Wilson's (2011) call for increased awareness and a less complex system. Current federal and state funding policies inhibit college access and completion for single mothers (Duquaine-Watson, 2007; Huelsman & Engle, 2013; Johnson, 2010; Radey & Cheatham, 2013).

Climate.   An institution's climate can positively or negatively influence single mothers' access and success. Climate refers to the "various structural aspects of the college and the behaviors of faculty, staff, and students" (Duquaine-Watson, 2007, p. 231). External factors can influence climate because they can alter the attitudes and behaviors of campus members toward students who are perceived as unwelcome or as if they are out of place in the college environment. The welfare reforms of the 1990s were designed to increase labor market participation among public assistance recipients, and single mothers who received benefits were more likely to be perceived as out of the norm on campus (Austin & McDermott, 2003; Costello, 2014; Duquaine-Watson, 2007).

Perceptions about who belongs in college influence structures within the environment, and single mothers' access to college can be dependent on structures that enable them to enroll and complete classes. Single mothers who experience lengthy waiting periods for access to on-campus child care, and have to go off campus to access day care, experience constrained finances, wasted time, and subsequent frustration. Single mothers may feel ignored or singled out because of their student-parent status or unwelcome on campus (Duquaine-Watson, 2007).

Other studies indicate that faculty, staff, and single mothers themselves can take steps to alleviate feeling unwelcome on campus. College support programs, supportive significant others, single-mother support groups, supportive faculty, on-campus child care and housing, and connections to healthcare and government resources can counteract single mothers' barriers to postsecondary access and completion (Austin & McDermott, 2003; Brown & Adansi, 2007; Bruns, 2004; Cerven, 2013; Lovell, 2014; Romo & Segura, 2010; Schumacher, 2015; Van Stone, Nelson, & Niemann, 1994).

Pedagogical and Classroom Experiences. Single mothers' perceptions of how they are treated in the classroom by peers and faculty can influence their sense of belonging and their desire to continue. Unwelcoming faculty or policies that cause barriers to successful course completion (i.e., mandating outside of class meetings or event attendance) deter persistence for single mothers (Duquaine-Watson, 2007; Lovell, 2014; Romo & Segura, 2010; Schumacher, 2015). Schumacher (2015) found that course delivery (i.e., online or hybrid environments) and positive interactions with faculty encouraged single mothers' persistence, a finding that is corroborated by other studies (Austin & McDermott, 2003; Duquaine-Watson, 2007; Romo & Segura, 2010). Small class sizes and faculty members who have an understanding of the challenges faced by single mothers have positive correlations with single mothers' decisions to continue postsecondary education (Austin & McDermott, 2003; Duquaine-Watson, 2007; Romo & Segura, 2010).

College Support Programs. Comprehensive college support programs play an important role for single mothers, and include application assistance, academic advising, tutoring, peer support, mentoring, and counseling (Cerven, 2013; Fenster, 2003; Romo & Segura, 2010; Schumacher, 2015). Single mothers often struggle with acquiring accurate information and advice regarding entry and persistence in postsecondary education; therefore, access to advisors, counselors, and other college support personnel can ease their challenges (Austin & McDermott, 2003; Brock & Richburg-Hayes, 2006; Brown & Adansi, 2007; Fenster, 2003; Matus-Grossman, Gooden, Wavelet, Diaz, & Seupersad, 2002; Richburg-Hays, 2008; Romo & Segura, 2010). Single mothers often lack time and may find it difficult to seek out support services, so connecting to student support services (i.e., academic counseling) yields positive outcomes for single mothers (Brock & Richburg-Hays, 2006; Matus-Grossman et al., 2002; Richburg-Hays, 2008; Romo & Segura, 2010; Schumacher, 2015). Matus-Grossman et al. (2002) found that comprehensive support systems increased students' awareness and feelings of connectedness to the institutions.

College support programs provide avenues for knowledge acquisition, communication, academic assistance, and ways in which single mothers can engage with their institutions (Austin & McDermott, 2003; Cerven, 2013; Fenster, 2003; Romo & Segura, 2010). Fenster (2003) investigated whether students receiving TANF benefits could achieve academic success if given proper supports, specifically tutoring, academic advising, preregistration, counseling, smaller class sizes, child care, and transportation reimbursement. The study compared the achievement (i.e., GPA in a 100-level psychology class, election to the dean's list, and rates of dismissal) of the TANF recipients and the general population of the community college. TANF students had higher GPAs, higher rates of election to the dean's list, and were equally likely to be dismissed for academic reasons as the general population. Multiple college support structures are necessary to the success of students receiving TANF benefits, because they not only provide needed services, they improve students' sense of belonging (Fenster, 2003).

Supportive Others.   Research clearly demonstrates single mothers' need to have support systems in their collegiate environment and in their personal lives (Austin & McDermott, 2003; Brown & Adansi, 2007; Bruns, 2004; Cerven, 2013; Costello, 2014; Duquaine-Watson, 2007; Romo & Segura, 2010; Schumacher, 2015; Van Stone, Nelson, & Niemann, 1994). Supportive others provide encouragement, assist with application processes, and act as referrals. Through an interview participant, Cerven (2013) demonstrates how single mothers rely on a network of supportive others to assist them with accessing college:

> Well, my sister helped me get enrolled and stuff, and then I had a friend who attended right after … she graduated (from high school) early and she started right after that. And so she helped me with any questions I had. Her mom helped me with applying. … (p. 10)

Supportive others also play a significant role in single mothers' persistence, as many need assurance and encouragement (Cerven, 2013; Costello, 2014; Schumacher, 2015; Van Stone et al., 1994). Costello (2014) notes that family member encouragement can positively influence pregnant and parenting teens' college access persistence.

Support groups can also positively influence single mothers' persistence (Austin & McDermott, 2003; Brock & Richburg-Hays, 2006; Brown & Adansi, 2007; Bruns, 2004; Cerven, 2013; Costello, 2014; Fenster, 2003; Richburg-Hays, 2008; Schumacher, 2015; Van Stone et al., 1994). Bruns

(2004) found that the single-mother support group provided an outlet for single mothers to discuss their challenges, receive peer assistance to overcome barriers, and feel connected with a community of other single mothers also pursuing postsecondary education. Support groups assist single mothers with balancing their multiple roles and helping them persist in higher education (Bruns, 2004; Schumacher, 2015).

Child Care.   Access to affordable and dependable child care is the most frequent need and concern cited by single mothers pursuing postsecondary education (e.g., Matus-Grossman et al., 2002; Schumacher, 2015). Campuses that provide reimbursement for child care or on-campus child care for single mothers positively influence their persistence (Matus-Grossman et al., 2002; Richburg-Hays, 2008; Romo & Segura, 2010; Schumacher, 2015). In contrast, a lack of affordable and dependable child care often inhibits participation and success in postsecondary education for single mothers (Cerven, 2013; Costello, 2014; Duquaine-Watson, 2007; Romo & Segura, 2010; Schumacher, 2015). Schumacher (2015) asserts that access to child care is a key strategy to helping single mothers access and complete higher education, and assistance can take the form of on-campus child care, child-care subsidies, assistance with finding child care, and partnerships with private organizations to provide assistance (Schumacher, 2015).

In summary, the environment profoundly influences single mothers' decisions to access and persist in postsecondary education. A lack of college support programs, the absence of supportive others, and unwelcoming climates create difficulties for single mothers. However, policies and practices that account for the unique characteristics of single mothers can encourage their access and completion (Austin & McDermott, 2003; Cerven, 2013; Richburg-Hays, 2008; Romo & Segura, 2010; Schumacher, 2015).

Postsecondary Outcomes for Single Mothers

Postsecondary education is a pathway for single mothers to escape poverty (Pandey et al., 2006; Zhan & Pandey, 2004a; 2004b). The most concrete outcome single mothers experience as a result of engaging in postsecondary education is reduced financial vulnerability through increased earning potential (Goldrick-Rab & Sorensen, 2010; Pandey et al., 2006; Radey & Cheatham, 2013; Zhan & Pandey, 2004a; 2004b). In examining the financial vulnerability of 770 single mothers, Pandey et al. (2006) found that 62% of single mothers with less than a high school degree were poor, compared to 6% of single mothers with a bachelor's degree. Further, of the nonpoor single mothers, 72% had bachelors' degrees. It is clear that economic mobility and decreased financial vulnerability are beneficial postsecondary outcomes for single mothers.

Other postsecondary outcomes for single mothers are increased family stability, higher educational aspirations for their children, increased parenting time, and increased well-being (Goldrick-Rab & Sorensen, 2010; Ricco, Sabet, & Clough, 2009). Goldrick-Rab and Sorensen (2010) found that college attendance assisted single mothers in forming networks of better-educated friends, resulting in higher educational expectations for their children and different decisions in their parenting practices. Similarly, Ricco et al. (2009) found that the role of student affected the role of parent, and mothers' attitudes toward their education served as a basis toward their children's attitudes toward education. Increasing children's educational aspirations is a transformative outcome of a single mother's pursuit of postsecondary education.

There are also important long-term implications for single mothers in their ongoing participation in higher education. The academic pipeline metaphor suggests that although women represent the majority of undergraduates, they "leak" out of the pipeline at later stages—especially in doctoral programs and as faculty members—and work and family conflicts are one reason for the leaks (e.g., Ward & Wolf-Wendel, 2012). The ideal worker norms that privilege some students over others can have long-term consequences for women and their choice to pursue ongoing education and academic careers (Austin, 2002). If single mothers perceive that academic environments are not conducive to their success, such ideas could persist into their decisions about whether to pursue graduate and professional degrees.

Recommendations and Implications for Practice

Single student mothers, like other high-risk populations, should be viewed holistically. There is no magic bullet that will make all of them successful. Instead, colleges and universities need to assist single student mothers in building a network of support through policy, collaboration, and student-centered strategies.

Revise Policy so that It Is Clear and Simple.   There are multiple resources available for single student mothers; however, these programs are often confusing and not clearly communicated. Many single mothers are ill-informed and/or do not understand the eligibility or application procedures to access and secure assistance. Low-income single mothers may not fill out the FAFSA, resulting in high levels of unmet need (Huelsman & Engle, 2013; Radey & Cheatham, 2013). Attending school part-time limits the eligibility of single mothers for full federal aid benefits. Federal and state financial aid policies and processes should be revised to promote simplicity and clarity (Wilson, 2011). Further, welfare policy and financial aid policies should be reviewed for inclusivity of student parents, especially single mothers (Goldrick-Rab & Sorensen, 2010; Johnson, 2010). Colleges and universities are in a unique position to advocate for single mothers, to revise current communication strategies surrounding federal and state aid and assistance programs, and to promote comprehensive services.

Postsecondary institutions should be well versed in policies and practices that can help accommodate single mothers' unique needs (Schumacher, 2015). Recruitment and outreach staff should be well trained on the policies and collaborations that could assist single mothers (Schumacher, 2015).

Promote Collaboration Between Community Organizations, State and Local Agencies, and Postsecondary Institutions. Single mothers are often eligible for a variety of benefit programs and resources provided through community agencies (Brock & Richburg-Hays, 2006; Richburg-Hays, 2008). Programs connecting community organizations and state and local agencies with institutions of postsecondary education have had success assisting single mothers (Richburg-Hayes, 2008; Romo & Segura, 2010; Schumacher, 2015). Colleges should pursue partnerships to build a network of support structures for single mothers.

Provide Child-Care Services or Assistance. The literature clearly outlines the concerns of single mothers regarding affordable and dependable child care (e.g., Goldrick-Rab & Sorensen, 2010; Duquaine-Watson, 2007). As the number of single mothers has grown on college campuses, the number of campus-based and campus-serving child-care centers has decreased (Institute for Women's Policy Research, 2016). Campuses that provide child-care assistance have higher rates of single mothers participating and persisting in higher education (Matus-Grossman et al., 2002; Richburg-Hays, 2008; Romo & Segura, 2010; Schumacher, 2015). Institutions should provide child-care assistance to single mothers (Schumacher, 2015).

Provide Comprehensive Support Services. Multiple studies showed increased persistence among single mothers who had access to comprehensive support services including counseling, academic support, and peer support groups (Austin & McDermott, 2003; Brown & Adansi, 2007; Bruns, 2004; Cerven, 2013; Costello, 2014; Romo & Segura, 2010). Institutions should implement extensive academic and personal support services, especially single-mother support groups (Austin & McDermott, 2003; Bruns, 2004; Romo & Segura, 2010; Schumacher, 2015). Such services help single mothers balance their multiple roles and increase their feelings of belonging (Schumacher, 2015).

Conclusion

Postsecondary access and completion is crucial for the economic and personal well-being of single mothers and their families (e.g., Goldrick-Rab & Sorensen, 2010). Using Astin's (1993) college impact model as a guide, this review focuses on single mothers and their experiences in accessing, persisting, and completing postsecondary education. The findings from the literature point to changes to policy and practice that can help support single mothers' success as students.

References

Astin, A. (1993). *What matters in college? Four critical years revisited.* San Francisco, CA: Jossey-Bass.

Austin, A. E. (2002). Preparing the new generation of faculty: Graduate school as socialization to the academic career. *The Journal of Higher Education, 73*(1), 94–122.

Austin, S., & McDermott, K. (2003). College persistence among single-mothers after welfare reform: An explanatory study. *Journal of College Student Retention, 5*(2), 93–113.

Brown, R., & Adansi, A. (2007). College females as mothers: Balancing the roles of student and motherhood. *The Association of Black Nursing Faculty Journal, 18*(1), 25–32.

Brock, T., & Richburg-Hayes, L. (2006). Paying for persistence: Early results of a Louisiana scholarship program for low-income parents attending community college. *Manpower Demonstration Research Corporation Opening Doors Project,* 1–46.

Bruns, D. (2004). Support groups for single-mothers in college. *The Academic Exchange Quarterly, 9*(4), 1–10.

Cerven, C. (2013). Public and private lives: Institutional structures and personal supports in low-income single-mothers' educational pursuits. *Educational Policy Analysis Archive, 21*(7), 1–29.

Costello, C. (2014). Pathways to postsecondary education for pregnant and parenting teens. *Working Paper for the Institute for Women's Policy Research Student Parent Success Initiative,* 1–54.

Duquaine-Watson, J. (2007). "Pretty darned cold": Single-mother students and the community college climate in post-welfare reform America. *Equity and Excellence in Education, 40*(3), 229–240.

Estes, D. K. (2011). Managing the student-parent dilemma: Mothers and fathers in higher education. *Symbolic Interaction, 34*(2), 198–219. doi:10.1525/si.2011.34.2.198

Fenster, J. (2003). Can welfare mothers hack it in college? A comparison of achievement between TANF recipients and general population community college students. *Journal of College Student Retention, 5*(4), 421–430.

Gault, B., Reichlin, L., Reynolds, E., & Froehner, M. (2014). 4.8 million college students are raising children. *Institute for Women's Policy Research Fact Sheet #C424,* 1–2.

Gault, B., Reichlin, L., & Roman, S. (2014). College affordability for low-income adults. *Institute for Women's Policy Research Policy Report #C412,* 1–43.

Goldrick-Rab, S., & Sorenson, K. (2010). Unmarried parents in college. *The Future of Children, 20*(2), 179–204.

Hochschild, A. (1989). *The second shift: Working parents and the revolution at home.* New York, NY: Viking.

Huelsman, M., & Engle, T. (2013). Student parents and financial aid. *Institute for Higher Education Policy,* 1–30.

Institute for Women's Policy Research (2016). Student parents' access to campus childcare continued to decline in 2015. Institute for Women's Policy Institute Quick Fact #Q051. http://www.iwpr.org/publications/recent-publications

Johnson, V. (2010). Impact of race and welfare reform on African American single-mothers access to higher education. *Journal of Black Studies, 40*(6), 1041–1051.

Lovell, E. (2014). College students who are parents need equitable services for retention. *Journal of College Student Retention, 16*(2), 187–202.

Matus-Grossman, L., Gooden, S., Wavelet, M., Diaz, M., & Seupersad, R. (2002). Opening doors: Students' perspectives on juggling work, family, and college. *Manpower Demonstration Research Corporation,* 1–123.

National Center for Education Statistics. (2002). *Nontraditional undergraduates,* Report by Susan Choy. Washington, DC: Author

National Center for Education Statistics. (2016). *Characteristics of postsecondary students.* Washington, DC: Author.

Nelson, B., Froehner, M., & Gault, B. (2013). College students with children are common and face many challenges in completing higher education. *Institute for Women's Policy Research Briefing Paper, IWPR#C404,* 1–5.

Osborne, M., Marks, A., & Turner, E. (2004). Becoming a mature student: How adult applicants weigh the advantages and disadvantages of higher education. *Higher Education: The International Journal of Higher Education and Educational Planning,* 48(3), 291–315.

Pandey, S., Zhan, M., & Kim, Y. (2006). Bachelor's degree for women with children: A promising pathway to poverty reduction. *Equal Opportunities International,* 25(7), 488–505.

Radey, M., & Cheatham, L. (2013). Do single-mothers take their share? FAFSA completion among aid-eligible female students. *Journal of Diversity in Higher Education,* 6(4), 261–275.

Ricco, R., Sabet, S., & Clough, C. (2009). College mothers in the dual roles of student and parent implications for their children's attitudes toward school. *Merrill-Palmer Quarterly,* 55(1), 79–110.

Romo, L., & Segura, D. (2010). Enhancing the resilience of young single-mothers of color: A review of programs and services. *Journal of Education for Students Placed at Risk,* 15(1–2), 173–185.

Richburg-Hays, L. (2008). Helping low-wage workers persist in education programs: Lessons from research on welfare training programs and two promising community college strategies. *Manpower Demonstration Research Corporation,* 1–26.

Schumacher, R. (2015). Supporting student parent success in postsecondary education. *Institute for Women's Policy Student Parent Success Initiative, IWPR #C406,* 1–5.

Van Stone, N., Nelson, J., & Niemann, J. (1994). Poor single-mother college students' views on the effect of some primary sociological and psychological belief factors on their academic success. *The Journal of Higher Education,* 65(5), 571–584.

Ward, K., & Wolf-Wendel, L. E. (2012). *Academic motherhood: Managing work and family.* New Brunswick, NJ: Rutgers University Press.

Wilsey, S. (2013). Comparisons of adult and traditional college-age student mothers: Reasons for college enrollment and views of how enrollment affects children. *Journal of College Student Development,* 54(2), 209–214.

Wilson, K. (2011). If not welfare, then what? How single-mothers finance college post-welfare reform. *Journal of Sociology and Social Welfare,* 38(4), 51–76.

Wolf-Wendel, L., & Ruel, M. (1999). Developing the whole student: The collegiate ideal. In D. Toma & A. Kezar (Eds.), *New directions for higher education: No. 105. Reconceptualizing the collegiate ideal* (pp. 35–46). San Francisco, CA: Jossey-Bass.

Zhan, M., & Pandey, S. (2004a). Economic well-being of single-mothers: Work-first or postsecondary education? *Journal of Sociology and Social Welfare,* 31(3), 87–112.

Zhan, M., & Pandey, S. (2004b). Postsecondary education and economic well-being of single-mothers and single fathers. *Journal of Marriage and Family,* 66(3), 661–673.

Sydney Beeler *is a doctoral student in the Department of Educational Leadership and Policy Studies at the University of Kansas, and currently serves as the Vice President of Enrollment Management at Westmoreland County Community College.*

6

This chapter focuses on graduate students who are parents, the career-related resources they gather during graduate school, and the influence of those resources on PhD-earning mothers' attainment of tenure-track faculty jobs at U.S. higher-education institutions.

The Effects of Parenthood During Graduate School on PhD Recipients' Paths to the Professoriate: A Focus on Motherhood

Amanda M. Kulp

The concept of the ideal worker as a workplace norm pervades the academic environment, and graduate student experiences are no exception (e.g., Hochschild, 1995). Visions of the ideal worker shape graduate students' behaviors as they seek to demonstrate to their professors and advisors that they are "good students" or truly committed to their fields of study (Brus, 2006). Graduate students often internalize unstated expectations that to be good students, they should play the role of worker bee in their departments, making themselves available at any time with any amount of notice (Estes, 2011; Lynch, 2008). Living up to this interpretation of the good student can be problematic for graduate students who are mothers, because it conflicts with cultural expectations that they also be good mothers, or intensive parents who are willing to sacrifice their own needs for their children (Espinoza, 2010; Estes, 2011; Lynch, 2008). Graduate-student mothers are less likely to become deeply socialized into academic departments and may be less likely to obtain key career-related resources, such as co-authorship of papers with advisors (Kennelly & Spalter-Roth, 2006). For mothers who seek to attain tenure-track faculty jobs after graduating with their terminal degrees, failure to accumulate these kinds of resources in graduate school may cause them to be at a disadvantage when

The author thanks the National Science Foundation and Donna Ginther of the University of Kansas for a site license to use the data. The use of NSF data does not imply NSF endorsement of the research, research methods, or conclusions contained in this report. Any errors are my own responsibility.

NEW DIRECTIONS FOR HIGHER EDUCATION, no. 176, Winter 2016 © 2016 Wiley Periodicals, Inc.
Published online in Wiley Online Library (wileyonlinelibrary.com) • DOI: 10.1002/he.20211

it comes to competing for jobs in the academic labor market (Kennelly & Spalter-Roth, 2006; Wolfinger, Mason, & Goulden, 2008).

This study focuses on graduate students who are mothers, the career-related resources they gather during graduate school, and the influence of those resources on PhD-earning mothers' attainment of tenure-track faculty jobs at U.S. higher-education institutions. This study compares PhD-earning mothers to other PhD-earning groups, including fathers who have children during graduate school and men and women who do not have children during graduate school. Analyzing data from the Survey of Earned Doctorates and the Survey of Doctorate Recipients by the National Science Foundation (NSF, 2014a; 2014b), this study focuses on PhD recipients who are U.S. citizens and who graduated from U.S. higher-education institutions between 2000 and 2005. Understanding whether and how PhD mothers "leak" out of the academic pipeline at the junction between graduate school and the professoriate is essential for higher-education institutions, researchers, and policy makers because doctoral students serve as valuable resources to higher-education institutions and ensure continued research and knowledge production. The effects of gender and family status on tenure-track faculty job attainment may also inform our understanding of persistent gender gaps in academia in terms of earning potential, job status, and mobility.

Background

Tenure-track faculty jobs are relatively scarce for new PhD recipients who seek them (e.g., Golde & Dore, 2001), which can be concerning for women who have children and pursue paths toward entry into the professoriate (e.g., Mason, 2013; Morrison, Rudd, & Nerad, 2011; Wolfinger et al., 2008; Wolfinger, Mason, & Goulden, 2009). Women with children under age 6 are 22% less likely than fathers and nonparents to attain tenure-track jobs straight out of graduate school (Mason, 2013; Wolfinger et al., 2008), and they take 29% longer than both fathers and nonparents to attain tenure-track jobs (Morrison et al., 2011). Women are overrepresented in part-time, non-tenure-track jobs, as they are 43% more likely than men to hold adjunct faculty positions (McMahon & Green, 2008).

The mismatch between career aspirations and available tenure-track positions for PhD-earning mothers has implications for the academic and scientific communities as well as for higher-education policy makers. A "leak" in the academic pipeline on the basis of gender and family status is especially concerning in science and engineering fields, where females are sorely underrepresented (Gibbs, McGready, Bennett, & Griffin, 2014; Kelly & Grant, 2012). Persistent gender gaps in academia in terms of earning potential, job status, and mobility may also be linked to the fact that PhD mothers are more negatively affected by parenthood and marriage than married men with children and single women without children (Jacobs, 2004;

Jacobs & Winslow, 2004a, 2004b; Lynch, 2008; Miller, 2009; Wolf-Wendel & Ward, 2006). It is important to understand how and why PhD mothers do not choose to pursue academic careers, whether and how they face a baby penalty, and if graduate-school factors influence PhD mothers' career paths (e.g., Mason, 2013).

Purpose and Theoretical Framework

This study examines PhD mothers' and others' accumulation of career-related resources in graduate school and how such accumulation influences their likelihood of attaining tenure-track faculty jobs within the first 8 to 13 years after PhD graduation. The term *PhD mothers* refers to women who parent children while in graduate school and who do or do not pursue faculty positions upon earning their terminal degrees. I compare mothers to (a) fathers in graduate school, (b) men without children in graduate school, and (c) women without children in graduate school.

This study uses cumulative advantage theory as a lens to understand PhD mothers' accumulation of career-related resources (DiPrete & Eirich, 2006; Merton, 1973, 1988). Cumulative advantage theory suggests that social status affects one's ability to secure resources over time, affecting long-term outcomes like employment and advancement for the individual (Merton, 1973, 1988). In this study, it is hypothesized that PhD recipients who accumulate resources early on or in greater quantities than others in graduate school tend to have a cumulative advantage in competing for tenure-track faculty jobs in the academic labor market (DiPrete & Eirich, 2006; Merton, 1973, 1988).

To measure PhD recipients' accumulation of career-related resources during graduate school, this study uses a conceptual framework constructed from two established frameworks: Enders' (2002) *Doctoral Professional Success* framework and Kennelly & Spalter-Roth's (2006) *Doctoral Career-Related Resources and Strategies* framework. This blended framework as represented in Figure 6.1 allows for an examination of the factors that represent resources that doctoral students attain in graduate school that assist them in competing for tenure-track faculty jobs.

Research Questions and Methods

This study investigated the following research questions:

1. To what extent have PhD-earning mothers attained tenure-track faculty jobs at US higher-education institutions within the first 8 to 13 consecutive years of earning their terminal degrees?
2. How do individual, institutional, doctoral training, and professional life-course factors differ among PhD-earning mothers, fathers, men without children, and women without children?

NEW DIRECTIONS FOR HIGHER EDUCATION • DOI: 10.1002/he

Figure 6.1. Conceptual Framework: Doctoral Career-Related Resources

Resources

Individual	Institutional
Age at time of PhD Married/partnered at time of PhD Number of dependents at time of PhD Age of dependents at time of PhD Time to PhD degree (in years) PhD academic discipline	Doctorate institutional type Doctorate institutional control Doctorate program ranking
Doctoral Training	**Professional Life Course**
Held a GTA position Held a GRA position Primary source of financing for graduate school attendance Research productivity during or in the first 2 years after graduate school as evidenced by journal articles published	Employment outside a GTA, GRA, or fellowship during graduate school Holding a postdoctoral job Holding a non-tenure-track faculty job after graduate school

I used a sample of doctoral recipients who earned PhDs between 2000 and 2005, who responded to the NSF (2014a) Survey of Earned Doctorates ($N = 2{,}994$), and who also responded to the Survey of Doctorate Recipients (SDR) between 2006 and 2013 (NSF, 2014b). I used logistic regression analyses that include the variables from the conceptual framework to determine how the career-related resources that PhD recipients accumulate in graduate school influence their comparative attainment of tenure-track faculty positions.

This study treats PhD graduation as an accumulation checkpoint, rather than measuring the incremental accumulation of career-related resources in a time series during graduate school (e.g., Merton, 1973). Although cumulative advantage is classically measured using such timing variables (e.g., DiPrete & Eirich, 2006; Merton, 1973), limitations in the available data prevented the measurement of the incremental accumulation of such resources during PhD recipients' graduate school years.

Findings

The sample ($N = 2{,}994$) was roughly divided between men at 47.9% and women at 52.1% (Table 6.1). Most respondents (84.6%) did not have children during graduate school. Only 214 female respondents (7.1%) and 248 male respondents (8.3%) had children during graduate school, graduated during the requisite years, and responded to the SDR between 2006 and 2013.

Table 6.1. Descriptive statistics: Independent variables (N = 2,994)

Independent Variables	Perc. (%)
Female	1,559 (52.1)
Male	1,435 (47.9)
Age 0–34 years	1,794 (59.9)
Age 35+	1,200 (40.1)
Married/partnered during grad school	1,116 (37.3)
Not married/partnered during grad school	1,878 (62.7)
No children during grad school	2,532 (84.6)
One child during grad school	388 (13.0)
More than one child during grad school	74 (2.5)
At least one child aged 0–5 during grad school	315 (10.5)
At least one child aged 6–18 during grad school	192 (6.4)
Time to PhD ≤ 10 yrs	2,539 (84.8)
Time to PhD>10 yrs	455 (15.2)
Natural sciences	1,328 (44.4)
Social sciences	1,100 (36.7)
Life sciences	253 (8.5)
Engineering	313 (10.5)
Research university (very high)	2,529 (84.5)
Research university (high)	312 (10.4)
Special focus/other institution	153 (5.1)
Public	2,086 (69.7)
USNWR Top-quartile ranked program	1,082 (36.1)
Held a GTA position	1,779 (59.4)
Held a GRA position	1,725 (57.6)
Primary funding: GRA	607 (20.3)
Primary funding: GTA	468 (15.6)
Primary funding: Fellowships, scholarships, grants	1,133 (37.8)
Primary funding: Self, family, or loans	786 (26.3)
Did not publish journal article during/after grad school	1,073 (35.8)
Published one journal article	289 (9.7)
Published more than one journal article	1,632 (54.5)
Held outside job during grad school	370 (12.4)
Held a postdoc	710 (23.7)
Held a non-tenure-track job	1,147 (38.3)

PhD mothers often came from the social sciences, graduated around age 38, and were 5 to 6 years older than their peers. Mothers took, on average, 1 year longer to graduate with their PhDs compared to the average PhD recipient. Mothers were more likely to graduate from research institutions, but fewer mothers graduated from top-ranked programs. Most mothers financed their degrees through personal funding and loans. They were about as productive as other groups in terms of publishing journal articles, and most of them published articles during or immediately after graduate school. Slightly fewer mothers held postdoctoral (postdoc) fellowships, but mothers were overrepresented in non-tenure-track faculty jobs.

NEW DIRECTIONS FOR HIGHER EDUCATION • DOI: 10.1002/he

Table 6.2. Tenure-track employment outcomes across gender and family status ($N = 2,994$)[§]

	Mothers	Women Without children	Fathers	Men Without children	χ^2
Attained a tenure-track job ≤ 2 years post-PhD	33.2	20.5	40.7	21.0	63.3[***]
Attained a tenure-track job at all 2006–2013	47.2	50.2	56.0	54.8	9.1
First employer:					
Research institution	43.0	38.0	35.5	43.1	90.6[***]
Doctoral	8.9	6.1	8.1	6.0	
Comprehensive	16.8	11.5	20.6	10.4	
Liberal arts	7.0	5.7	6.9	4.5	
2-year institution	3.3	2.9	6.9	1.9	
Special focus	5.1	5.2	6.9	3.6	

[§]*Due to the small N in some groups, percentages rather than frequencies are reported.*
Note. ***$p \le .001$, **$p \le .01$, *$p \le .05$

Descriptive Findings.   Descriptively, fathers and mothers who had children during graduate school attained tenure-track jobs in higher percentages at earlier rates than their peers who did not have children during graduate school (Table 6.2). These findings complicate the existing literature on PhD mothers, which suggests that mothers experience up to a 22% delay in attaining tenure-track faculty jobs (Morrison et al., 2011; Wolfinger et al., 2008). However, when compared in the regressions with men without children in graduate school and considering the entire observation period of 2006 to 2013, mothers fell short of attaining tenure-track jobs in comparable percentages to other groups. This finding aligns with the existing literature, which suggests that mothers experience a gender penalty and a baby penalty and have lower overall rates of tenure-track job attainment compared to other groups (e.g., Mason, 2013).

Mothers who had children in graduate school were more evenly distributed across employer institutional type and more often worked at nonresearch institutions including comprehensive, liberal arts, 2-year, and special-focus institutions than at research universities.

The descriptive findings suggest that because mothers accumulate different sorts of funding and support from their programs than other groups, they are at a cumulative disadvantage when it comes to competing for highly valued jobs at research institutions (e.g., DiFuccia, Pelton, & Sica, 2007;

Table 6.3. Logistic regression on career related resources influencing tenure-track job attainment for PhD recipients by comparison group (N = 2,994)

	Had children during graduate school		Did not have children during graduate school	
	Mothers	Fathers	Men	Women
Married/partnered	1.33	1.48	1.11	0.97
35+ years old	1.10	1.25	0.86	1.27
Time to PhD 10+ years	1.32	1.45	0.79	0.81
Natural sciences (ref)				
Social sciences	5.14**	2.56*	2.32***	4.12**
Life sciences	2.57	18.73**	2.79**	1.96***
Engineering	7.54	1.66	1.15	0.81*
Research university (very high) (ref)	–	–	–	–
Research university (high)	0.29	2.16	.87	0.79
Special focus/other	0.40	2.38	.49	0.38**
Public institution	1.14	1.34	1.02	1.13
Top 25 ranked program	0.58	2.82*	1.14	1.12
Held a GRA position	1.36	2.00	1.44*	1.98
Held a GTA position	0.61	1.42	1.22	1.36*
Primary Funding: GRA (ref)	–	–	–	–
Primary Funding: GTA	0.51	1.43	1.63	1.70
Primary Funding: Scholarship, fellowship	0.40	1.75	1.18	1.30
Primary Funding: Self, family, loan	0.20*	0.95	0.95	1.06
Published 0 articles (ref)	–	–	–	–
Published 1 article	0.97	0.67	0.69	0.96
Published > 1 article	1.49	1.55	1.73**	1.65
Outside job	0.91	0.86	1.01	1.04
Postdoc	0.30*	0.13***	0.14***	0.18***
Non-tenure-track faculty	0.09***	0.05***	0.10***	0.10***
−2 Log Likelihood	202.13	225.65	1,184.04	1,375.28
Chi-square (df = 20)	88.86***	114.52***	447.34***	489.26***
Overall percentage	79.4%	79.4%	77.7%	77.0%
Nagelkerke R^2	0.45	0.50	0.42	0.41
N	214	248	1,187	1,345

Note. ***$p < 0.001$, ***$p < 0.01$, *$p < 0.05$. Values reported are odds ratios [Exp(B)].

Hollenshead, Sullivan, Smith, August, & Hamilton, 2005; Kulis, Sicotte, & Collins, 2002; Wolfinger et al., 2009).

Tenure-Track Predictors.   The regression models conducted for PhD mothers, PhD men without children, PhD women without children, and PhD fathers showed that the estimations of the models were significant ($p < .001$) (Table 6.3). The overall percentages from the mothers, fathers, men without children, and women without children regression models were

79.0%, 79.4%, 77.7%, and 77.0%, respectively. The Nagelkerke R2 were 0.456, 0.496, and 0.420, and 0.407, respectively, indicating that the models explained 45.6% of the variance in tenure-track attainment for mothers; 49.6% of the variance in tenure-track attainment for fathers; 42.0% of the variance in tenure-track attainment for men without children; and 40.7% of the variance in tenure-track attainment for women without children.

Previous studies have found that the career-related resources in the conceptual framework influence doctoral recipients' likelihood of attaining tenure-track faculty jobs (Enders, 2002; Kennelly & Spalter-Roth, 2006), but this study found that the only shared significant predictors across all groups were academic discipline, holding a non-tenure-track faculty job, and holding a postdoctoral position. Institutional type, being in a top-ranked program, financing one's degree through a teaching assistantship, and publishing articles in or shortly after graduate school all mattered variably for members of other groups, but not for PhD mothers. Financing one's degree through self, family, or loan sources was the only significant covariate that specifically influenced PhD mothers' likelihood of attaining tenure-track jobs, and it negatively influenced their odds of tenure-track job attainment.

Individual Variables.   For mothers, being in the social sciences positively predicted attaining a tenure-track job, because social-science mothers had over 5 times greater odds of attaining a tenure-track faculty job (odds ratio = 5.142, $p < .01$) than natural-sciences mothers. Being in a social-science field also benefited other groups: Men without children in graduate school and fathers in graduate school each had about 2.5 times greater odds of attaining tenure-track faculty jobs (odds ratio for men without children = 2.450, $p < .001$; odds ratio for fathers = 2.893, $p < .05$), and women who did not have children during graduate school had about 1.5 times greater odds of attaining tenure-track jobs (odds ratio = 1.732, $p < .01$) than their natural-sciences counterparts. Being in the life sciences benefited men without children in graduate school (odds ratio = 2.782, $p < .01$) and fathers in graduate school (odds ratio = 16.761, $p < .01$), and being in an engineering field benefited women without children in graduate school (odds ratio = 3.935, $p < .05$).

Institutional Variables.   Mothers had no significant institutional predictors of tenure-track job attainment. Men and women in graduate school who had no children and who graduated from institutions with a Carnegie 2010 classification of "research university (very high)" had 2 times greater odds of attaining tenure-track jobs (inverse odds of 0.436, $p < .05$ for men without children, and inverse odds of 0.368, $p < .01$) as PhD recipients who graduated from "special focus" institutions. Graduating from a *US News and World Report* top-25-ranked program was significant for fathers, as fathers who graduated from such programs had over 2.5 greater odds of attaining tenure-track jobs (odds ratio = 2.620, $p < .05$) than fathers who did not graduate from top-ranked programs.

New Directions for Higher Education • DOI: 10.1002/he

Doctoral Training Variables. Mothers who funded their degrees through research assistantships rather than primarily through self, family, or loan sources had 5 times greater odds of attaining a tenure-track job (inverse odds of .198, $p < .01$). Women without children in graduate school who financed their degrees primarily through a teaching assistantship had nearly 2 times greater odds to attain a tenure-track job (odds ratio $= 1.88,7$, $p < .01$) than those who financed their degrees through a research assistantship. Publishing more than one article in graduate school or shortly thereafter was a significant predictor for men and women without children in graduate school, but not for fathers and mothers. Men and women without children who published more than one article had over 1.5 times greater odds to attain tenure-track faculty jobs (odds ratio $= 1.687$, $p < .01$ for men without children; odds ratio $= 1.656$, $p < .01$ for women without children) than those who published no articles.

Professional Life-Course Variables.   Across all models, holding a postdoctoral fellowship significantly reduced one's chances of attaining a tenure-track job. PhD mothers who did not hold postdocs had nearly 3.5 times greater odds of attaining a tenure-track job than those who did hold postdocs (inverse odds ratio of 0.303, $p < .05$). Women without children in graduate school who did not take postdocs had 5 times greater odds of attaining tenure-track jobs than those who did take postdocs (inverse odds ratio of .175, $p < .001$). Men in graduate school without children and fathers who did not take postdocs had 7 times greater odds of attaining tenure-track jobs than those who did take postdocs (inverse odds ratio of 0.140, $p < .001$ for men without children; inverse odds ratio of 0.142, $p < .001$ for fathers). These findings support recent studies that suggest, despite the expectations, many postdocs seem to have of moving on to the tenure track (e.g., Powell, 2014; Yamamoto, 2014), taking a postdoc lowers the odds of attaining tenure-track jobs.

Similarly, holding a non-tenure-track job negatively influenced one's chances of attaining a tenure-track job. PhD mothers who did not hold non-tenure-track jobs had 11 times greater odds of attaining a tenure-track job than those who did hold non-tenure-track jobs (inverse odds of 0.091, $p < .001$). Fathers in graduate school who did not hold non-tenure-track jobs had 21 times greater odds of attaining a tenure-track job than those who took such jobs (inverse odds ratio of 0.047, $p < .001$). Men and women without children in graduate school who did not hold non-tenure-track faculty jobs had nearly 10 times greater odds of attaining a tenure-track faculty job (inverse odds ratio of 0.101, $p < .001$ for men; inverse odds ratio of 0.094, $p < .001$ for women) than those who held non-tenure-track positions. These findings correspond with studies suggesting non-tenure-track jobs provide poor stepping-stones for those hoping to move on to the tenure-track (Coalition on the Academic Workforce, 2012; Kezar & Sam, 2010).

Discussion

The "conventional wisdom" in academia advises faculty-bound women against having children in graduate school, recommending they delay family formation even until the point of achieving tenure (e.g., Kennelly & Spalter-Roth, 2006; Lynch, 2008; Mason, 2013; Morrison et al., 2011; Sallee, 2011; Wolfinger et al., 2008; 2009). However, the findings from this study suggest that this conventional wisdom may not always be true. There are a variety of reasons that might explain why PhD mothers fared better in this study than in previous studies.

Changing Attitudes Toward Balancing Academic Work and Life. Mothers in this sample may have been influenced by broadly changing attitudes toward balancing academic work and family life for newer generations of faculty members (e.g., Helms, 2010; Trower, 2010; Wolf-Wendel & Ward, 2015). The mothers in this study may be among the recent generations of academic women who seek to "have it all" with family and work (Helms, 2010; Trower, 2010; Wolf-Wendel & Ward, 2015, p. 28). Academic women who employ strategies and take advantage of institutional supports to manage academic and family responsibilities can and do experience productive academic lives and fulfilling family lives (e.g., Ward & Wolf-Wendel, 2012).

Disciplinary Differences. Mothers in this study may have attained tenure-track jobs at higher rates because they were concentrated in the social sciences, which have become feminized in the sense that faculty hiring opportunities for women have vastly improved in recent decades (Kalleberg & Reskin, 1995; Morrison et al., 2011; Spalter-Roth & Merola, 2001). That being said, some fields have experienced more gender parity in faculty hiring than others (Ginther & Kahn, 2006; Van Vooren & Spalter-Roth, 2008). Also, women in science, technology, engineering, and mathematics (STEM) fields often strongly identify with their professional fields and may seek career options other than academia (Mason, 2013; Monosson, 2008). A larger number of job opportunities and a relatively weaker pull from the professional realm may have allowed mothers in the social sciences to match to faculty jobs more easily.

Mothers in Graduate School Are Relatively Rare. Very few women have children in graduate school despite the fact that those that are doing so are going on to attain tenure-track jobs at higher rates than some other groups. This study did not address *why* the number of PhD mothers continues to be quite small. Graduate women may be "leaning in" to academic work by dedicating themselves to their academic pursuits above other life priorities (Sandberg, 2013). Mothers who plan to seek academic positions may be developing strategies to handle real and perceived potential familial conflicts in ways that allow them to successfully accommodate the simultaneously demanding roles of mother and student (e.g., van Anders, 2004; Wolfinger et al., 2008). It is also possible that recent cohorts of PhD mothers are benefiting from institutional policies that are helping them graduate and attain tenure-track jobs.

New Directions for Higher Education • DOI: 10.1002/he

Mothers Take Jobs at Different Types of Institutions.   Gender and family status affected employer institutional type. Women were generally less likely than men to attain jobs at research (very high) institutions, and PhD mothers were less likely than women without children to attain jobs at research institutions. In this way, the gendered effect on the institutional type of one's employer was compounded for mothers, as both gender and family status negatively influenced their likelihood of securing jobs at research institutions (Wolf-Wendel & Ward, 2006).

The data in this study do not indicate whether mothers failed to secure jobs at research-focused institutions or self-selected away from jobs at research-focused institutions, but previous literature suggests that both activities may be at play (e.g., Bair & Haworth, 2004; Gardner, 2008; Ginther & Kahn, 2006; Mason, 2013; Wolf-Wendel & Ward, 2006). Departmental norms in more male-dominated fields may shape hiring committees' perceptions in considering mothers to be good candidates for tenure-track positions (DiFuccia et al., 2007; Kulis et al., 2002; Ginther & Kahn, 2006).

Women with children may self-select away from jobs at research-oriented institutions because they perceive incompatibilities between keeping up with research productivity expectations for tenure and the demands of family life (Bair & Haworth, 2004; Gardner, 2008; Ginther & Kahn, 2006; Mason, 2013). These women may not realize that research universities offer a number of built-in supports (e.g., abbreviated teaching loads, graduate students) to help them maintain active scholarship records. Teaching-oriented institutions typically do not offer this level of research support, despite expecting increased research productivity (e.g., Ward & Wolf-Wendel, 2012).

Perhaps more mothers seek jobs at more teaching-oriented institutions simply because they enjoy teaching (e.g., Bair & Haworth, 2004; Gardner, 2008; Mason, 2013; Wolf-Wendel & Ward, 2006). In this way, greater numbers of mothers may be seeking jobs at institutions in noncompeting segments of the academic labor market (Burke, 1988; Clark, 2014; Finnegan, 1993; Twombly, 2005).

Professional Experiences Are Important.   This study supports previous literature suggesting that the academic pipeline metaphor is too restrictive to accurately describe the path of PhD mothers (Cannady, Greenwald, & Harris, 2014; Pawley & Hoegh, 2011). The metaphor of a continuous pipeline from graduate school to the professoriate assumes that nontenure-track faculty jobs or postdocs may eventually lead to tenure-track jobs as PhD mothers move from one stage to the next in a linear path. However, the pipeline metaphor does not account for the fact that postdocs are leading PhD mothers away from, rather than toward, the tenure track.

Limitations.   The factors in the conceptual framework chosen for this study failed to fully explain the variance in PhD mothers' attainment of tenure-track jobs, so we cannot fully determine whether differences in accumulation of these career-related resources put PhD mothers at a cumulative disadvantage compared to other groups. The tenure-track employment outcomes for PhD mothers suggest the opposite. This study was primarily concerned with whether PhD mothers attained tenure-track jobs in comparable quantities to others, and despite their small numbers and differences in types of employers, PhD mothers were successful in attaining these jobs. Although there were differences in the accumulation of career-related resources between PhD mothers and others, these differences did not come to bear on the equations modeling tenure-track job attainment. The inability of this study to use SDR data to pin down the observable variables that explain PhD mothers' attainment of tenure-track jobs is a challenge that other studies have also observed (e.g., Ginther & Kahn, 2006).

Importance of the Study

This study extends current research threads on faculty careers and PhD recipients' employment patterns by offering up-to-date analyses on the employment patterns of PhD recipients and by offering specific analyses on the academic employment patterns of PhD recipients (e.g., Rhoades & Torres-Olave, 2015). This study also addresses a current gap in the higher-education literature on whether and how PhD recipients with different individual and graduate school characteristics are filtered into tenure-track jobs in the primary academic labor market and into non-tenure-track jobs in the secondary academic labor market (Kezar & Sam, 2010; Rhoades, 2013; Rhoades & Torres-Olave, 2015). Contributions from this study inform researchers, higher-education institutions, policy makers, and current and potential graduate students by helping them understand the influences on preparation for the successful leap from graduate student to assistant professor.

Conclusion

This study examined the effects of gender and family status on PhD recipients' likelihood of attaining tenure-track faculty jobs at U.S. higher-education institutions, with a specific focus on PhD mothers who have children during graduate school. This study found that recent cohorts of PhD mothers attain tenure-track jobs in higher percentages and at earlier points than men and women without children. Higher-than-average numbers of mothers pursue academic jobs, so the graduate school factors that help them shape their career aspirations and secure tenure-track positions are key to understanding the recent trends in job outcomes for mothers.

PhD mothers are valuable resources to higher-education institutions and current tenure-track faculty in research and knowledge production. Persistent gender gaps in terms of earning potential, promotion potential, job status, and mobility affect PhD mothers' job attainment. It is important for higher-education faculty, administrators, and policy makers to understand the graduate school factors that influence PhD mothers' career path realities. This study identified patterns, trends, and previously unidentified relationships between graduate school and the professoriate for PhD mothers. These relationships should prompt higher-education researchers to continue to study PhD mothers and their early career pathways to and away from the tenure-track.

References

Bair, C., & Haworth, J. (2004). Doctoral student attrition and persistence: A metasynthesis of research. In J. C. Smart (Ed.), *Higher education: Handbook of theory and research* (pp. 481–534). Dordrecht, The Netherlands: Kluwer Academic.

Brus, C. P. (2006). Seeking balance in graduate school: A realistic expectation or a dangerous dilemma? In M. Guentzel & B. Nesheim (Eds.), *New directions for student services: No. 115. Supporting graduate and professional students: The role of student affairs* (pp. 1–45). San Francisco, CA: Jossey-Bass.

Burke, D. (1988). *A new academic marketplace*. Westport, CT: Greenwood Press.

Cannady, M. A., Greenwald, E., & Harris, K. N. (2014). Problematizing the STEM pipeline metaphor: Is the STEM pipeline metaphor serving our students and the STEM workforce? *Science Education, 98*(3), 443–460.

Clark, B. (1987). *The academic life: Small worlds, different worlds*. Princeton, NJ: Carnegie Foundation for the Advancement of Teaching.

Coalition on the Academic Workforce (CAW). (2012). *A portrait of part-time faculty members*. Washington, DC: Coalition on the Academic Workforce. Retrieved from: http://www.academicworkforce.org/CAW_portrait_2012.pdf

DiFuccia, M., Pelton, J., & Sica, A. (2007). If and when sociology becomes a female preserve. *The American Sociologist, 38*, 3–22.

DiPrete, T. A., & Eirich, G. M. (2006). Cumulative advantage as a mechanism for inequality: A review of theoretical and empirical developments. *Annual Review of Sociology, 32*, 271–297.

Enders, J. (2002). Serving many masters: The PhD on the labour market, the everlasting need of inequality, and the premature death of Humboldt. *Higher Education, 44*, 493–517.

Espinoza, R. (2010). The good daughter dilemma: Latinas managing family and school demands. *Journal of Hispanic Higher Education, 9*(4), 317–330.

Estes, D. K. (2011). Managing the student-parent dilemma: Mothers and fathers in higher education. *Symbolic Interaction, 34*(2), 198–219.

Finnegan, D. E. (1993). Segmentation in the academic labor market: Hiring cohorts in comprehensive universities. *The Journal of Higher Education, 64*(6), 621–656.

Gardner, S. K. (2008). Student and faculty attributions of attrition in high and low-completing doctoral programs in the United States. *Higher Education, 58*(1), 97–112.

Gibbs, K. D., Jr., McGready, J. B., Bennett, J. C., & Griffin, K. (2014). Biomedical science PhD career interest patterns by race/ethnicity and gender. *PLoS ONE, 9*(12), e114736.

Ginther, D. K., & Kahn, S. (2006). *Women's careers in academic social science: Progress, pitfalls, and plateaus*. Working Paper. Boston, MA: Boston University.

Golde, C. M., & Dore, T. M. (2001). *At cross purposes: What the experiences of doctoral students reveal about doctoral education*. A report prepared for The Pew Charitable Trusts. Philadelphia, PA.

Helms, R. M. (2010). *New challenges, new priorities: The experience of generation X faculty. A study for the collaborative on academic careers in higher education*. Cambridge, MA: Harvard Graduate School of Education.

NEW DIRECTIONS FOR HIGHER EDUCATION • DOI: 10.1002/he

Hochschild, A. R. (1995). The culture of politics: Traditional, postmodern, cold-modern, and warm-modern ideals of care. *Social Politics, 2,* 331–346.

Hollenshead, C. S., Sullivan, B., Smith, G. C., August, L., & Hamilton, S. (2005). Work/family policies in higher education: Survey data and case studies in policy implementation. In J. W. Curtis (Ed.), *New directions for higher education: No. 130. The challenge of balancing faculty careers and family work* (pp. 41–65). San Francisco, CA: Jossey-Bass.

Jacobs, J. A. (2004). The faculty time divide. *Sociological Forum, 19*(1), 3–27.

Jacobs, J. A., & Winslow, S. E. (2004a). The academic life course, time pressures, and gender inequality. *Community Work and Family, 7*(2), 143–161.

Jacobs, J. A., & Winslow, S. E. (2004b). Overworked faculty: Job stresses and family demands. *Annals: American Academy of Political and Social Science, 596,* 104–129.

Kalleberg, A. L., & Reskin, B. (1995). Gender differences in promotion in the United States and Norway. *Research in Social Stratification and Mobility, 14,* 237–264.

Kelly, K., & Grant, L. (2012). Penalties and premiums: The impact of gender, marriage, and parenthood on faculty salaries in STEM and non-STEM Fields. *Social Studies of Science, 42,* 872–899

Kennelly, I., & Spalter-Roth, R. M. (2006). Parents on the job market: Resources and strategies that help sociologists obtain tenure-track jobs. *American Sociologist, 3*(4), 29–49.

Kezar, A., & Sam, C. (2010). Understanding the new majority of non-tenure-track faculty in higher education. *ASHE Higher Education Report, 36*(4). San Francisco, CA: Jossey-Bass.

Kulis, S., Sicotte, D., & Collins, D. (2002). Women scientists in academia: Geographically constrained to big cities, college clusters, or the coasts? *Research in Higher Education, 43,* 1–30.

Lynch, K. D. (2008). Gender roles and the American academe: A case study of graduate student mothers. *Gender and Education, 20*(6), 585–605.

Mason, M. A. (2013). *Do babies matter? Gender and family in the ivory tower.* New Brunswick, NJ: Rutgers University Press.

McMahon, D., & Green, A. (2008). Gender, contingent labor, and writing studies. *Academe, 94*(6), 16–19.

Merton, R. K. (1973). The Matthew effect in science. In N. W. Storer (Ed.), *Sociology of science.* Chicago IL: University of Chicago Press.

Merton, R. K. (1988). The Matthew effect in science, ii: Cumulative advantage and the symbolism of intellectual property. *Isis, 79,* 606–623.

Miller, A. R. (2009). The effects of motherhood timing on career path. *Journal of Population Economics, 24*(3), 1071–1100.

Monosson, E. (Ed.) (2008). *Motherhood, the elephant in the laboratory: Women scientists speak out.* Ithaca, NY: Cornell University Press.

Morrison, E., Rudd, E., & Nerad, M. (2011). Onto, up, off the academic faculty ladder: The gendered effects of family on career transitions for a cohort of social science PhDs. *The Review of Higher Education, 34*(4), 525–553.

National Science Foundation. (2014a). Survey of Earned Doctorates. Retrieved from: www.nsf.gov/statistics/srvydoctorates/

National Science Foundation. (2014b). Survey of Doctorate Recipients. Retrieved from: www.nsf.gov/statistics/srvydoctoratework/

Pawley, A. L., & Hoegh, J. (2011). *Research brief: Exploding pipelines: Mythological metaphors structuring diversity-oriented engineering education research agendas.* Paper presented at the ASEE Annual Conference. Vancouver, Canada.

Powell, K. (2014, August 22). The transferrable postdoc. *Science, 342*(6199), 956–959.

Rhoades, G., & Torres-Olave, B. M. (2015) Academic capitalism and (secondary) ALMs: Negotiating a new academy and research agenda. In M. B. Paulsen (Ed.), *Higher education: Handbook of theory and research* (vol. 30, pp. 383–430). Dordrecht: Springer.

Rhoades, G. (2013). Disruptive innovations for adjunct faculty: Common sense for the common good. *Thought & Action, 29*(Fall), 71–86.

Sallee, M. W. (2011). Performing masculinity: Considering gender in doctoral student socialization. *Journal of Higher Education, 82*(2), 187–216.

Sandberg, S. (2013). *Lean in: Women, work and the will to leave.* New York, NY: Knopf.

Spalter-Roth, R., & Merola, S. (2001, August). *Early career pathways: Differences among moms and dads, childless men, and childless women in sociology.* Paper presented at the annual meeting of the American Sociology Association. Anaheim, CA.

Trower, C. (2010). A new generation of faculty: Similar core values in a different world. *Peer Review, 12*(3), 27–30.

Twombly, S. B. (2005). Values, policies, and practices affecting the hiring process for full time arts and sciences faculty in community colleges. *Journal of Higher Education, 76*(4), 423–447.

vanAnders, S. M. (2004). Why the academic pipeline leaks: Fewer men than women perceive barriers to becoming professors. *Sex Roles, 51*(9–10), 511–521.

Van Vooren, N., & Spalter-Roth, R. (2008). Success of women with children in sociology. *Footnotes, 36*(8), 1. Retrieved from www.sanet.org/footnotes/nov08/women

Ward, K., & Wolf-Wendel, L. E. (2012). *Academic motherhood: Managing work and family.* New Brunswick, NJ: Rutgers University Press.

Wolf-Wendel, L., & Ward, K. (2006). Academic life and motherhood: Variations by institutional type. *Higher Education, 52*(3), 487–521.

Wolf-Wendel, L., & Ward, K. (2015). Academic mothers: Exploring disciplinary perspectives. *Innovative Higher Education, 40*(1), 19–35.

Wolfinger, N. H., Mason, M. A., & Goulden, M. (2008). Problems in the pipeline: Gender, marriage, and fertility in the ivory tower. *The Journal of Higher Education, 79*(4), 388–405.

Wolfinger, N. H., Mason, M. A., & Goulden, M. (2009). Stay in the game: Gender, family formation and alternative trajectories in the academic life course. *Social Forces, 87*(3), 1591–1621.

Yamamoto, K. (2014). Time to rethink graduate and postdoc education. *iBioMagazine.* Retrieved from www.ibiology.org/ibiomagazine/issue-11-keith-yamamoto-time-to-rethink-graduate-and-postdoc-education.html

AMANDA M. KULP is a program manager in the office of institutional research and planning at the University of Kansas.

7

This chapter describes the themes that emerged in this volume with attention to important policy implications on the federal, state, and institutional levels. Recommendations for future research are provided.

Complexity of Work-Life Identities and Policy Development: Implications for Work-Life in Higher Education

Jaime Lester

In 2008, I arrived at George Mason University (GMU) with a book monograph completed on family-friendly policies in higher education (Lester & Sallee, 2009) and much knowledge on the most effective policies and practices to support work-life in higher-education institutions. My level of hope for the development of work-life across the enterprise of higher education was high and my dedication steadfast. Fast-forward 8 long years to 2016, and GMU just implemented a one-semester paid family and medical-leave policy for faculty. You may ask why it took 8 years for a higher-education organizational-change scholar with deep knowledge on work-life policies and practices to effect change, particularly in developing a policy that is common on many college campuses. My response is simple: Change in higher education is wrought with difficulties, and work-life balance is among one of the more complex gender-based issues that challenges the very foundation of work and the sociological relationship between work and family. The purpose of this concluding chapter is to provide a synthesis of themes across the chapters and to offer implications for policy development and practices on the federal, state, and institutional level.

The chapters in this volume provide a wealth of information that extends knowledge and conceptualizations of work-life in higher education. What is revealed across the chapters is an acknowledgment of the multifaceted and abstract nature of the ideal-worker phenomenon. Acker (1990), along with Williams (2000), introduced the very conceptualization of organizations as gendered, noting that every aspect of organizational life— "advantage and disadvantage, exploitation and control, action and emotion, meaning, and identity" (Acker, 1990, p. 146)—are defined through

NEW DIRECTIONS FOR HIGHER EDUCATION, no. 176, Winter 2016   © 2016 Wiley Periodicals, Inc.
Published online in Wiley Online Library (wileyonlinelibrary.com) • DOI: 10.1002/he.20212

a distinction between masculine and feminine. The "ideal worker" is most clearly defined by Williams (2000) as "... someone who works at least 40 hours a week year round. This ideal-worker norm, framed around the traditional life patterns of men, excludes most mothers of childbearing age" (p. 2). Williams argues that the very structure of society with families as the primary unit creates a systemic disadvantage for women, particularly in the workplace, where they are often expected to behave like their male counterparts who historically have a support network (often a wife) in the home who cares for all domestic needs. As continuously noted across all the chapters, the ideal-worker expectations are directly challenged by women who entered higher-education as students and in the workforce in larger numbers and now by men who are resisting traditional notions of masculinity and desiring more influence and time with their children and families. The ideal-worker notion has been used across the higher-education literature (see Erickson, 2012; Gardner, 2013; Lester, 2008; Slaughter, 2001); but, as suggested by Lester, Sallee, and Hart (in press), much of this work has failed to incorporate the comprehensive nature of the concept and often focuses on gender as a binary—women/feminine or men/masculine.

A major critique of the literature that motivated this very volume is the historical focus on women and parenting in the academy. Arguably, this area of inquiry was an important place to begin to examine work-life because early work on women faculty highlighted stark gender salary inequities that were justified by the prevailing assumption that women faculty with children were less productive than men (Cole & Zuckerman, 1987; Hamovitch & Morgenstern, 1977; Perna, 2001; Sax, Hagedorn, Arredondo, & Dicrisi, 2002). The research by Ward and Wolf-Wendel (2004, 2012), Armenti (2004), Drago et al. (2006), and Mason, Goulden, and Wolfinger (2006) revealed the complex nature of parenting in the academy for faculty and graduate students, sparking debate and eventually policy change. Now, one of the major themes across these chapters is a need to look beyond parenting and to begin a discourse on work-life as an issue of health, caring for aging parents, and balance for all, including those individuals without children.

A related theme found across these chapters is a need to complicate work-life beyond conversations of gender—masculine and feminine—to a more intersectional view of identities. Research on work-life has often separated the experiences of women and men with little analysis of other identities salient in institutional and sociological contexts. What is needed is to understand how gender, race, socioeconomic status, sexuality, and the like intersect to reveal new areas of understanding of work-life in higher education. Ward and Wolf-Wendel in Chapter 1 on midcareer faculty begin this conversation with acknowledgment that all faculty groups—men and women—need to be included in discussions of leadership, mentorship, and bias. In addition, the other identities that lead to qualitatively difference experiences with work-life need to be addressed building on the work on faculty of color, transgender, and social class in the academy.

New Directions for Higher Education • DOI: 10.1002/he

Another contribution and theme across the chapters is the deep examination of how local institutional norms shape work-life balance experiences for individuals or constituent groups. The literature on work-life in higher education has shown that the academic department plays a strong role in the ways in which individuals are or are not able to experience work-life balance. In this volume, Wilk in Chapter 3 contrasts the administrative expectations in student affairs and instructional technology units. She identifies the primary role that supervisors play in allowing for more work-life balance via flexible work schedules and the norms around accessing and responding to emails and other work communications outside of normal work hours. Kulp in Chapter 6 concludes that PhD mothers may fare better on the faculty job market due to their disciplinary affiliation in the social sciences. She also identifies the differences across institutional types, noting that PhD mothers tend to begin their faculty careers in more teaching-focused institutions. Kezar and Bernstein in Chapter 2 note that non-tenure-track faculty members are frequently left out of the discussion altogether, despite frequently having intense work-life needs. Finally, both Sallee in Chapter 4 and Beeler in Chapter 5 note that undergraduate and graduate programs are not entirely friendly to student parents. Both recommend additional attention to accommodate those students who are balancing (or juggling) work, parenting, and school. Each of these analyses provides additional evidence of the complex nature of work-life and the impact that the unit or department has on the ability to achieve work-life balance.

Recommendations

The research on work-life in higher education has outlined a series of recommendations for ways to address the ideal worker phenomenon. However, the focus to date has been primarily on tenure-track faculty members who are mothers of young children—only one set of workers in higher-education institutions. Here, I outline several recommendations at the national, state, and institutional level.

Work-Life on the National Stage. The current policy context for work-life across the United States and within institutions of higher education is minimal with very few paid-leave options and little consistency across institutions and state lines. Therefore, the most impactful change that could be made to address work-life in higher education institutions would be to revise the Federal Family and Medical Leave Act.

The Obama Administration has for several years promoted the Healthy Families Act, which offers up to 7 paid sick days per year for each employee (White House, 2015, para 8). Other initiatives promoted by the Obama Administration related to work-life include increasing wages, providing overtime pay, offering affordable health insurance, and providing equal pay for women. In 2015, the Family and Medical Insurance Leave Act (FAMILY)

NEW DIRECTIONS FOR HIGHER EDUCATION • DOI: 10.1002/he

was introduced to provide up to 12 weeks of paid leave. Although this act was not passed, national advocacy groups—National Partnership for Women and Families, Working Mother, and A Better Balance—continue to promote paid leave. In addition to the recommendations, national advocacy groups, particularly those associated with historically disenfranchised groups in higher education such as contingent faculty and graduate students, can play a role in promoting a more inclusive FMLA to address those who are contingent by employment classification. Graduate students, for example, are not considered employees despite the fact that many of them receive their entire income in part-time jobs as research or teaching assistants. Without protections from the FMLA, they have no job security or medical insurance protections during or after a family or medical event.

Another recommendation is for the federal government, in partnership with other higher-educational national organizations, to resurrect and revise the former National Center for Education Statistics National Study of Postsecondary Faculty Survey (NSOPF). Since the elimination of NSOPF, no other national survey captures large-scale data on faculty including information on how faculty spend their time, the differences across faculty groups (contingent versus tenure-track), and measures such as those related to work-life balance. Aligned with the arguments set forth in this volume, the newly designed NSOPF should also include other university employees to include staff, student affairs administrators, and wage employees. A compliment to these data would be additional measures on national faculty surveys used by the Survey of Doctorate Recipients (see Chapter 5) or the Harvard Collaborative on Academic Careers in Higher Education (COACHE) group to more precisely examine work-life measures and career pathways.

State-Level Implications.   One of the major roles that states need to consider are the restrictions placed on family and medical leave policies for all state employees regardless of their organizational contexts. In many states, 12-month staff and administrator contracts are bound to the leave policies established at the state level, often aligned with the Federal FMLA, which guarantees only up to 12 weeks of unpaid leave for a family or medical event. Twelve-month staff and administrators may often use sick and/or vacation time or disability benefits via health insurance tied to retirement funds for paid leave. Higher-education institutions have their proverbial hands tied when it comes to providing additional paid leave for 12-month employees. Although I do suggest a modification to the FMLA that could address these concerns, states are also advised to provide additional leeway to colleges and universities that function not on a traditional schedule but rather on an academic schedule. I found (Lester, 2013) that the hierarchy embedded in employment contracts within colleges and universities was emphasized when faculty became eligible for a full semester of paid leave for family or medical reasons and other 12-month employees, especially staff, received lesser leave options.

States also have the ability to play an advocacy role with the federal government, to extend existing medical or leave benefits through negotiation with corporations and to creatively encourage collaborations between private and public entities and higher-education institutions that create or support work-life programs. State legislatures have the ability and power to create state-level legislation to support additional work-life programs. California, New Jersey, and Rhode Island, for example, offer a paid family-leave program integrated into disability insurance and paid for through payroll deductions. These types of programs not only offer additional immediate support for individuals and families, but they also can begin to put pressure at the federal level to revise the FMLA.

Colleges and universities will continue to face resource shortages in the form of lower state appropriations as well as criticism for raising tuition too steeply. States have the opportunity to help higher-education institutions by providing opportunities for collaborations for work-life benefits. These collaborations can include contracts for child-care facilities or stipends to access community-based child-care facilities, renegotiating disability benefits for state employees to include paid leave, creating healthy employee programming support through state funds, and adding payroll deductions to ensure paid leave programs for all employees.

Work-Life in Institutions of Higher Education. One important implication that emerged from this volume is the need to expand policies and practices for work-life balance to a diversity of populations—tenured and non-tenured faculty, staff, administrators, graduate students, and undergraduate students. As Kulp points out in Chapter 6, PhD mothers have been successful at obtaining tenure-track positions and should not be discouraged from a career path into the professoriate. Yet, only a handful of institutions provide any job protections for graduate students who experience a family or medical event. Many of the policies outlined in the American Association of University Professors' (2001) *Statement of Principles on Family Responsibilities and Academic Work* apply to graduate students as well as to pretenured faculty members and could be modified to support graduate students with children. Policies that assist with family demands including leaves of absence, deferred funding, health-insurance coverage, lactation support, access to affordable day care, and family leave, would provide needed support to graduate students who have children (Hollenshead, Sullivan, Smith, August, & Hamilton, 2005; Kuperberg, 2009; Lynch, 2008). The development of policies is particularly important in light of the consistent finding that departmental culture has a high impact on the support structures for PhD mothers, faculty mothers, and administrators. Institutions also need to pay attention to the needs of undergraduate parents—who form the first step into the academic pipeline.

The academic department or unit plays a primary role in the experience of work-life balance across employment contracts. As noted by each author in this volume, the department/unit defines acceptable social norms around work-life issues from childbearing, child-rearing, self-care, and care for aging parents. Social norms dictate how work-life balance is defined, who is eligible, and how to interpret the nuance of policy. Therefore, institutions need to continue to consider ways to impact department-level climate and norms and to address caregiver bias (Hochschild, 1995; Mason, 2013), unequal distribution of resources (Kennelly & Spalter-Roth, 2006), and a lack of socialization (Sallee, 2011). The development of new departmental practices and expectations do vary by constituent group. For graduate students, Kulp in Chapter 6 argues that faculty should mentor mothers and should assist them in publishing journal articles (Rhoades & Torres-Olave, 2015). Faculty and administrators should recommend wider access to resources such as research and teaching assistantships for graduate students who are mothers, so that graduate teaching assistantships, graduate research assistantships, fellowships, scholarships, and grants can also be primary funding sources for student mothers and other students who do not have children (Ehrenberg & Mavros, 1995; Ehrenberg, Rizzo, & Jakubson, 2007; Kim & Otts, 2010). Faculty and administrators should encourage PhD mothers to consider working at all types of institutions, as they do for PhD students with no children (Bair & Haworth, 2004; Gardner, 2008; van Anders, 2004). Finally, institutions should inform graduate students that taking a postdoctoral fellowship or a non-tenure-track faculty job may not ultimately lead them to the tenure track (Kezar & Sam, 2010). Sallee in Chapter 4 offers similar suggestions with a focus on single graduate-student parents to include the following: creating minicohorts of nontraditional students, developing classroom pedagogy that does not place undue burden on student parents outside of class, and more family-friendly events with programs and/or child care for children to allow student-parents to become part of the departmental and collegiate community.

The academic department and wider campus community also need to consider faculty programs and policies beyond stopping the tenure clock and taking a term-length leave to address work-life needs. These two programs tend to address the work-life needs for early career faculty—those faculty who are at childbearing age and are at the assistant professor rank. The research on midcareer faculty (Austin, 2010; Baldwin, DeZure, Shaw, & Moretto, 2008; Mathews, 2014; Trower, 2011), for example, provides evidence of a more complex set of considerations for midcareer faculty. In Chapter 1, Ward and Wolf-Wendel suggest that midcareer faculty need support via mentorship that offers career guidance, leadership development programs to support faculty who are in, or interested in, administrative roles, and updated campus policies that provide both pathways and recognition for mid-career faculty who are working to achieve the full professor rank. Continuing the same practices and policies only continues to support the idea of the ideal worker and to place women faculty and other groups at a disadvantage. What is needed is a direct challenge to the implicit bias evident in the ideal-worker phenomenon through policy development and implicit bias training.

Conclusion

This volume represents a deepening of the research on work-life in higher education by providing evidence for the diverse work-life needs of multiple constituent groups found on college campuses. Whether it be midcareer faculty, contingent faculty members, PhD students, single-parent undergraduates, master's students, or administrators, work-life is a goal that is not fully supported within higher education. To move forward, federal and state advocacy groups and legislatures need to consider new or revised policies that create a more encompassing view of who is eligible for paid family and medical leave and to be more aware of employees' work-life needs associated with caring for aging parents, medical issues, and personal aging. Additional research is needed that examines these needs across institutional types and employment contracts. Questions still remain on the work-life needs for contingent faculty, undergraduate students, and those at nonresearch universities. Very little is known about work-life in community colleges beyond the work of Ward, Wolf-Wendel, and Twombly (2007). More evaluative and quasi-experimental studies are needed on the impact of existing work-life policies and programs: How does a "family-friendly" campus impact undergraduates who are parents? How does term leave (semester or quarter) impact a faculty member's career? What are best practices with regard to contingent faculty members who have work-life concerns? These analyses and others need to be attentive to the intersection of identities and how those identities complicate notions of the ideal work. Lester, Sallee, and Hart (in press) note that the lack of intersectionality in research on the ideal worker masks how opportunities are limited for women, people of color, and those men whose behaviors run counter to traditional notions of masculinity. There are many opportunities to further the research on work-life, and we hope that this volume serves as a call to action.

References

Acker, J. (1990). Hierarchies, jobs, bodies: A theory of gendered organizations. *Gender and Society*, 4(2), 139–158.

American Association of University Professors. (2001). *Statement of principles of family responsibilities and academic work*. Retrieved 7/11/2016 from https://www.aaup.org/report/statement-principles-family-responsibilities-and-academic-work

Armenti, C. (2004). May babies and post tenure babies: Maternal decisions of women professors. *The Review of Higher Education*, 27(2), 211–231.

Austin, A. (2010). Supporting faculty members across their careers. In K. J. Gillespie & D. L. Robertson (Eds.), *A guide to faculty development* (2nd ed., pp. 363–378). San Francisco, CA: Jossey-Bass.

Bair, C., & Haworth, J. (2004). Doctoral student attrition and persistence: A meta-synthesis of research. In J. C. Smart (Ed.), *Higher education: Handbook of theory and research* (pp. 481–534). Dordrecht, The Netherlands: Kluwer Academic.

Baldwin, R., DeZure, D., Shaw, A., & Moretto, K. (2008). Mapping the terrain of mid-career faculty at a research university: Implications for faculty and academic leaders. *Change, 40*(5), 46–55.

Cole, J. R., & Zuckerman, H. (1987). Marriage, motherhood and research performance in science. *Scientific American, 256*(2), 119–125.

Drago, R., Colbeck, C. L., Stauffer, K. D., Pirretti, A., Burkum, K., Fazioli, J.,. . . Habasevich, J. (2006). The avoidance of bias against caregiving: The case of academic faculty. *American Behavioral Scientist, 49*, 1222–1247.

Erickson, S. K. (2012). Women Ph.D. students in engineering and a nuanced terrain: Avoiding and revealing gender. *The Review of Higher Education, 35*(3), 355–374.

Ehrenberg, R. G., & Mavros, P. G. (1995). Do doctoral students' financial support patterns affect their time-to-degree and completion rates? *Journal of Human Resources, 30*, 581–610.

Ehrenberg, R. G., Rizzo, M. J., & Jakubson, G. H. (2007). Who bears the growing cost of science at universities? In P. E. Stephen & R. G. Ehrenberg (Eds.), *Science and the university* (pp. 19–35). Madison: University of Wisconsin Press.

Gardner, S. K. (2008). Student and faculty attributions of attrition in high and low-completing doctoral programs in the United States. *Higher Education, 58*(1), 97–112.

Gardner, S. K. (2013). Women faculty departures from a striving institution: Between a rock and a hard place. *Review of Higher Education, 36*(3), 349–370.

Hamovitch, W., & Morgenstern, R. D. (1977). Children and the productivity of academic women. *The Journal of Higher Education, 48*(6), 633–645.

Hochschild, A. R. (1995). The culture of politics: Traditional, postmodern, cold-modern, and warm-modern ideals of care. *Social Politics, 2*, 331–346.

Hollenshead, C. S., Sullivan, B., Smith, G. C., August, L., & Hamilton, S. (2005). Work/family policies in higher education: Survey data and case studies in policy implementation. In J. W. Curtis (Ed.), New directions for higher education: No. 130. The challenge of balancing faculty careers and family work (pp. 41–65). San Francisco, CA: Jossey-Bass.

Kennelly, I., & Spalter-Roth, R. M. (2006). Parents on the job market: Resources and strategies that help sociologists attain tenure-track jobs. *The American Sociologist, 37*(4), 29–49.

Kezar, A., & Sam, C. (2010). Understanding the new majority of non-tenure-track faculty in higher education—demographics, experiences, and plans of action. *ASHE Higher Education Report, 36*(4).

Kim, D., & Otts, C. (2010). The effect of loans on time to doctorate degree: Differences by race/ethnicity, field of study, and institutional characteristics. *The Journal of Higher Education, 81*(1), 1–32.

Kuperberg, A. (2009). Motherhood and graduate education: 1970–2000. *Population Research and Policy Review, 28*(4), 473–504.

Lester, J. (2008). Performing gender in the workplace: Gender socialization, power, and identity among women faculty. *Community College Review, 34*(4), 277–305.

Lester, J. (2013). Work-life balance and cultural change: A narrative of eligibility. *Review of Higher Education, 36*(4), 463–488.

Lester, J., & Sallee, M. (2009). (Eds.). *Establishing a family-friendly campus: Bestpractices.* Sterling, VA: Stylus.

Lester, J., Sallee, M., & Hart, J. (in press). Beyond gendered universities? Implications for research on gender in organizations. *NASPA Journal About Women in Higher Education.*

Lynch, K. D. (2008). Gender roles and the American academe: A case study of graduate student mothers. *Gender and Education, 20*(6), 585–605.

Mason, M. A. (2013). *Do babies matter?: Gender and family in the ivory tower*. New Brunswick, NJ: Rutgers University Press.

Mason, M. A., Goulden, M., & Wolfinger, N. H. (2006). Babies matter: Pushing the equity revolution forward. In S. J. Bracken, J. K. Allen, & D. R. Dean (Eds.), *The balancing act: Gendered perspectives in faculty roles and work lives* (pp. 9–30). Sterling, VA: Stylus.

Mathews, K. R. (2014). *Perspectives on midcareer faculty and advice for supporting them*. Cambridge, MA: The Collaborative on Academic Careers in Higher Education.

Perna, L. W. (2001). The relationship between family responsibilities and employment status among college and university faculty. *The Journal of Higher Education*, 72(5), 584–611.

Rhoades, G., & Torres-Olave, B. M. (2015). Academic capitalism and (secondary) ALMs: Negotiating a new academy and research agenda. In M. B. Paulsen (Ed.), *Higher education: Handbook of theory and research* (vol. 30, pp. 383–430). Dordrecht: Springer.

Sallee, M. W. (2011). Performing masculinity: Considering gender in doctoral student socialization. *The Journal of Higher Education*, 82(2), 187–216.

Sax, L. J., Hagedorn, L. S., Arredondo, M., & Dicrisi, F. A. III. (2002). Faculty research productivity: Exploring the role of gender and family-related factors. *Research in Higher Education*, 43(4), 423–446.

Slaughter, S. (2001). Problems in comparative higher education: Political economy, political sociology and postmodernism. *Higher Education*, 41(4), 389–412.

Trower, C. A. (2011). Senior faculty satisfaction: Perceptions of associate and full professors at seven public research universities. *TIAA-CREF Institute Research Dialogue*, 101, 1–15.

van Anders, S. M. (2004). Why the academic pipeline leaks: Fewer men than women perceive barriers to becoming professors. *Sex Roles*, 51(9–10), 511–521.

Ward, K., & Wolf-Wendel, L. (2004). Academic motherhood: Managing complex roles in research universities. *The Review of Higher Education*, 27(2), 233–257.

Ward, K., & Wolf-Wendel, L. (2012). *Academic motherhood: How faculty manage work and family*. New Brunswick, NJ: Rutgers University Press.

Ward, K.A., Wolf-Wendel, L.E., & Twombly, S. B. (2007). Faculty life at community colleges: The perspective of women with children. *Community College Review*, 34(4), 255–281.

White House. (2015). Fact sheet: Helping middle-class families get ahead by expanding paid sick leave. Retrieved from https://www.whitehouse.gov/the-press-office/2015/09/07/fact-sheet-helping-middle-class-families-get-ahead-expanding-paid-sick

Williams, J. (2000). *Unbending gender: Why family and work conflict and what to do about it*. New York, NY: Oxford University Press.

JAIME LESTER is an associate professor of higher education at George Mason University.

Index